op

75-

THE ART OF
Bedouin Jewellery

A SAUDI ARABIAN PROFILE

THE ART OF
Bedouin Jewellery

A SAUDI ARABIAN PROFILE

Heather Colyer Ross

arabesque

The Art of Bedouin Jewellery
First published in 1981 by
Arabesque Commercial SA
1 Rue Fries, 1701 Fribourg
Switzerland

© 1981 Heather Colyer Ross
ISBN 0 907513 01 8

Phototypeset in Palatino by
Tradespools Limited, Frome, England
Printed in the Netherlands by
Royal Smeets Offset BV, Weert

Photography Heather Colyer Ross
except those pictures credited to Frank Cox
Design and production Anthony Nelthorpe MSIAD
in collaboration with Arabesque Commercial SA
Colour illustrations Jean Bowcott

Page 1: *Many pieces of Bedouin jewellery come to rest in the Kingdom of Saudi Arabia because they are sold when pilgrims progress annually toward Mecca. This style of bracelet has made its appearance in the women's souq in Riyadh within the last three years. Many pairs have now been purchased there. It seems likely that traders sought them to boost the growing demand for Bedouin jewellery. Most examples support small silver discs set above loops of applied filigree – in this pair, the discs are well-worn Ethiopian coins and provide a clue to the origin of the bracelets.*

Pages 2 and 3: *The most characteristic feature of Bedouin jewellery is perhaps its large size. The jnad is probably the largest piece. It is a unique style of necklace – designed to be worn around the neck and under one arm. The huge bells jangle with the slightest movement. Around Arabia, women claim that they wear such an ornament for dancing. A similar piece exists in Oman and this is worn by women under their clothes in the belief that it will aid fertility.*

Contents

Acknowledgements

In expressing my appreciation to the many people who have helped me to produce this book, my thanks naturally go first to those who assisted me with my first book, *Bedouin Jewellery in Saudi Arabia*, because it is upon that foundation my new work was accomplished.

Throughout the project of introducing Arabian Bedouin jewellery, I have received constant encouragment from Dr. Fouad Abdul-Salam al Farsy, the Deputy Minister of Industry, Kingdom of Saudi Arabia. Dr. Farsy is deeply interested in such facets of Arabian culture and always finds time to advise. Professor Abd al-Rahman al-Ansary, Chairman of the Archeology Department, Faculty of Arts, University of Riyadh, was also wonderfully co-operative in making information available. Dr. Abdulaziz H. al-Sowayyegh, Assistant Deputy Minister of Information, made it possible for this book to be published and I offer my thanks.

I am grateful to Mrs. Genevieve Puyraimond who took time away from completing her own book to discuss regional differences evident in Peninsula jewellery many years ago. Mrs. Suad Juffali was generous with her time, too, and gave me access to her fine collection of Bedouin jewellery, as did Mrs. Perry Omar Aggad. Khalid Racy also contributed his knowledge and jewellery collection for photographing. For these friends, and the others who helped in so many ways – especially Mary-Margaret McLernon, I hope my book is a sufficient tribute.

Working behind the scenes were Khalil Ghindi, Angela Cooke, Tony and Margie Nelthorpe, and my best friend, my husband Barry, who has supported me in my creative endeavours since we first met in 1959. I am most sincerely grateful for all the help I have received.

Heather Colyer Ross

6

Author's Note

Since writing my first book, *Bedouin Jewellery in Saudi Arabia*, I have met many fellow enthusiasts – a few of whom began collecting Bedouin jewellery in Saudi Arabia many years ago. They are most encouraging about this project and very helpful in allowing me to photograph rare or fine examples of traditional styles. Because of their interest in, and appreciation of my work, and requests from new collectors, it seems timely to provide a more comprehensive set of pictures with the additional information that has come to light about jewellery made and worn on the Arabian Peninsula.

New archaeological discoveries have been made within the Kingdom of Saudi Arabia and I have made a few of my own. There remains the hope that more facts will emerge to satisfy all those who are as intrigued as I am with this area of traditional life. Archaeology will ultimately provide many answers to our questions about the history of Arabian jewellery. Books about the subject are helpful, too. Since the publication of my first book in 1978, old memories have been stirred and interest awakened in the people of the Arabian Peninsula. Requests have been made for exhibitions and for the presentation of slide shows about the craft of Bedouin jewellery and subsequently, the public has come to realize the full extent of the range. As more exhibitions are planned, this new book may be helpful.

Compiling the book has been difficult only in that it is hard to select which pieces of jewellery help best to tell a story. Some of the pieces shown on these pages were made outside the Peninsula and came to rest in Saudi Arabia when their owners sold them so it is difficult to award provence in many cases. After the annual pilgrimage, unusual pieces can always be found at the Women's *souq* and this evidence suggests that inhabitants of other desert regions within the Muslim world sell jewellery to meet their expenses on the *Haj*.

One of the initial purposes of writing about Bedouin jewellery was to draw attention to a neglected subject and an important facet of Arabian culture. I also wanted my work to be both enjoyable and informative. I sincerely hope that these primary aims are fulfilled with this new book.

Heather Colyer Ross

Heather Colyer Ross
Riyadh
SEPTEMBER 1981

Foreword

Saudi Arabians and friendly Westerners, alike, have often expressed concern about the potentially negative effect of expatriate life-styles on Saudi Arabian cultural and social traditions. Such concern is sincere, well-meaning and of value as a way of urging the importance of maintaining the integrity of the Saudi Arabian ethos. Every day, however, there is more evidence that such concern betrays an underestimation of the tensile strength and elastic vitality of the uniquely Islamic culture, social bonds and everyday practice of Saudi Arabian people.

People concerned about Saudi Arabian culture should look to the entirely positive contributions resulting from the currently intensive interaction between Saudi Arabian citizens and visitors and workers from the world beyond our borders. When the current, dramatic, historic moment of Saudi Arabia is measured, any tendency to discount the many contributions of non-Saudi Arabians to the realization of our objectives would distort the full picture.

Saudi Arabian readers of Mrs. Heather Colyer Ross's Bedouin Jewellery in Saudi Arabia *will immediately recognize the positive potential inherent in Saudi Arabia's transactions with talented, disciplined and well-meaning non-Saudi Arabians. Built around the nearly infinite variety of types and styles of Bedouin women's jewellery, this book presented valuable insights into Bedouin history, land, social structure and way of life.*

The photographic representation of carefully selected pieces of Bedouin jewellery received immediate acclaim upon the publication of the book in 1978. But the even deeper value of this fine author's work lay in her in-depth inquiry into the varying historical influences of other countries' peoples on Bedouin life.

In the present offering, The Art of Bedouin Jewellery, *the newly created and already faithful audience of Mrs. Colyer Ross's first work will not be disappointed. The writing of this recent compendium of Bedouin jewellery gave the author an opportunity to open still wider the door to the rich world of this little known art form.*

Again, we are urged to go beyond the immediate pleasure of the photography or even the well written and carefully documented commentary. Nor, for that matter, should we limit our appraisal to the fact that the book, in itself, makes the survival of Bedouin Art all the more likely.

The book is, in its very appearance at this time, an artifact of the impact of Saudi Arabian life and culture on an increasingly curious, interested, and often delighted outside world. This book, like the one that preceded it, is yet another small window through which the depth, beauty, and richly durable Saudi Arabian culture can be witnessed and for those with eyes to see, can be appreciated.

Dr. Fouad Abdul-Salam al Farsy
Deputy Minister for Industry
Kingdom of Saudi Arabia
SEPTEMBER 1981

Introduction

Personal adornment is part of nature's plan. This is evidenced in the multiple hues of birds and beasts and by the designs traced on their bodies. Even trees and flowers attest to it. The purpose is to attract. A tree, shrub or plant is dressed in flowers to ensure the reproduction of the species, and so it is with animals.

As it is the male of the species that has the advantages, it is interesting to learn that men once wore more body ornamentation than women. Only quite recently, wives took over the role of conveying men's wealth and success by wearing the family jewellery. Elizabeth I of England, who inherited her father's love of lavish ornamentation, changed the fashion for the English. A French courtesan altered the course of jewellery custom on the European continent, when she borrowed and wore diamonds to catch the eye of a king.

Since the earliest history, jewellery and gems have been hoarded as wealth, and wealth, it is said, like courage, has to be shown off in some way. After the Renaissance, when men were left with only buttons, buckles and rings for adornment, the prestige derived from owning fabulous jewellery fell upon women. In supplying their wives with jewellery, men may be responding to a primitive urge to display.

In some parts of the world today, men still paint their bodies with bright colours and deck themselves out elaborately with feathers and ornaments. In Oriental lands, the custom of wearing jewellery was usually shared equally between men and women until relatively recent times, when women took over the role almost completely.

Jewellery is one of the oldest forms of decorative art and the exciting aspect of this is that most primitive features remain important to jewellery design today. Whereas man's recognition of the intrinsic beauty of certain materials and minerals led them to be the basis of his treasured ornaments, it is worthwhile to ponder the constant use of many of these by totally unconnected civilizations separated by vast barriers of time and space. For instance, turquoise is similarly treasured in both Arabia and America's south-west. That it is possible to trace how certain jewellery styles came to be transferred from one civilization to another is encouraging, yet there are still many gaps in the history of body ornament, particularly Arabian.

Only time and diligent research will provide the missing links in the meshed chains of jewellery history. At present, on the Arabian Peninsula, excavations have revealed many exciting clues. As yet, these are not fully documented – nor are the archaeological sites completely investigated. The bronze tools, crucibles, beads and gems retrieved from the earth thus far, promise to provide further instalments in the story of Arabian jewellery. Until the world is supplied with more facts, the subject of Bedouin jewellery must rely on the evidence provided by pieces existing today and the myriad of clues supplied by historians, explorers, Arabists, adventurers, archaeologists and enthusiasts.

Archaeology has revealed, so far, that man has always ornamented his body, which suggests the desire for self adornment is profound. The pretty stones found in the cave of "Peking man" supply evidence to confirm that the appreciation of gemstones goes far back in prehistory. It seems that, since the dawn of civilization, the possession of gems and wearing of jewellery have alleviated three of man's basic insecurities – vanity, superstition and a desire for material wealth. Special importance has been placed on jewellery, for it is associated with all the things with which man is most concerned: money, power, religion and love. While jewellery's basic function is to adorn, the reasons for which individuals bedeck themselves varies in the extent to which these factors are involved.

In time, jewellery became a form of currency. It is also known that, since prehistoric times, jewellery has had religious significance or superstitious associations. Ancient peoples wore amuletic jewellery to protect themselves against misfortunes and the displeasure of their gods in the belief that these ornaments possessed magical powers. In more recent times, jewellery often incorporated religious symbols or inscriptions in praise of deities. Today, most people wear religious, amuletic or symbolic ornaments of some kind and these attest to the continuing depth of jewellery's meaning for man.

Jewellery has often been used as a badge indicating rank or worth, especially among primitive peoples. Men of the nomadic African Danakil tribe are entitled to wear an ear-ring or bracelet as an alternative to a specially coloured loincloth or a feather or comb in their hair. A Danakil man's standing among his people depends on his reputation as a warrior – the number of men he has killed in battle or in a fair fight – and these marks of rank indicate how many lives he has taken.

The jewellery of early man was undoubtedly limited to such as nuts, dead beetles, shells, pebbles and so on, but in time, when his creations showed distinct artistic development, the lapidary craft was born. It was eventually followed by metal-working techniques.

The criteria for jewellery since time immemorial is that it must be both beautiful and precious; hence, the patrons of the craft have traditionally been the wealthy. Today, everyone is able to own some form of jewellery, even if it is only a wrist watch – although some regard a watch merely as a functional necessity, it is invariably chosen for its appearance as well as for its usefulness. Yet, even now, fine jewellery remains the most obvious expression of status and wealth because rare and expensive materials are almost always used in its manufacture; and the prices of the handicrafted pieces have been affected by escalating production costs.

Social change and mass-production techniques may have allowed everybody to possess jewellery, but, rich or poor, the reasons for wearing jewel adornments remain constant. The universal motives may be attributable to the Bedouin woman, too. Naturally she is proud of her jewellery which proclaims her a woman of property and makes her secure in the knowledge that she has negotiable savings of her own. Most of the ornaments were given to her on the occasion of her marriage as personal treasure. It is likely that the jewellery has romantic connotations, too, and she would be sentimental about it. However, it is important to record that, in the case of an Arabian woman, tradition is of primary importance in the acquisition and wearing of jewellery.

The Historical Background

In ancient times, the Arabian Peninsula was "the gateway to the East", and derived fabulous wealth from its location along important trade routes and from its commercial activities. Its prosperity is well documented.

As a land of abundance, south-western Arabia was known to the Romans as Arabia Felix, "contented" or "fortunate" Arabia. Perhaps it was contented because it enjoyed a peaceful existence. Archaeologists have found that its cities were unfortified. This calm existence may have been due to the comparative isolation of most towns. It was fortunate in that southern Arabia was the source of the finest *boukhor* (frankincense) and *morr* (myrrh). These rare aromatic resins were highly prized by the ancient world. During Roman times, it was customary to burn frankincense in temples and on the funeral pyres of royal and noble persons, whereas myrrh was used primarily in cosmetics, perfumes, medicaments and as an embalming agent. Because the demand for frankincense and myrrh was great and the supplies limited, the price was driven up, until, in biblical times, they were as expensive as gold.

Southern Arabia also traded in spices, silks, ivory and other valuable commodities destined for Egypt and the Mediterranian lands. Since consumers had no first-hand knowledge of the sources of these goods (India, East Africa and the Far East), Arabia carried on a highly profitable trade. Arabia also supplied the northern countries of the Near East with gold, copper, and precious stones. Some of this gold and copper came from rich mines within Arabia. Southern and western Arabia were also well known as a source of semi-precious stones.

Although the subject is debated, many scholars believe that the Semitic migration to southern Arabia and the beginnings of major trade in frankincense and myrrh coincided with the domestication of the camel. It seems logical that this significant development (generally set at 1400 BC,) would make travel and the transportation of cargo over vast stretches of arid lands possible. In any case, it is agreed that the anatomical limitations of the camel dictated the course of the trade routes. The camel is exceptionally top heavy when loaded and its feet are not suited to rocky ground. It is not an affective beast of burden in mountainous regions, so the best camel routes followed relatively level ground.

These ancient caravan routes can be traced across the plateaux and through the valleys to the east of the high mountains of south-western Arabia. Under heavy guard, the camels were formed into long trains that carried the rich cargoes. They became a spectacular and familiar part of the early Arabian scene. Caravaneers, drawn from different tribes, were careful to maintain a friendly neutrality with tribesmen whose territory they crossed.

Frankincense and myrrh were also transported by sea. In the ninth century BC, the fleet of Solomon, under Phoenician management, is believed to have transported these commodities to the Fertile Crescent. Throughout the first millenium BC, Arab vessels carried their precious cargo eastward to the Arabian Gulf and northward via the Red Sea to Egypt.

Although many caravan routes remain in use to the present day, the prosperity of the area was destined to come to an end. The economic decline of Arabia began in the first century BC, with an invasion by the covetous Romans. In time, Arabia's trading monopoly was destroyed when both the Greeks and Romans acquired the Arabs' navigational skills and learned the secrets of the monsoon winds. Some historians, however, calculate the beginning of southern Arabia's economic decline as late as the fourth century AD. It is sure that many factors contributed. Undoubtedly, the greatest economic loss was suffered when the frankincense market collapsed. The Roman Emperor Constantine, who embraced Christianity in 323 AD, proclaimed it the state religion of the Roman Empire; thereafter, simpler burials became popular and the demand for frankincense and myrrh decreased. The flow of wealth in reciprocal trade to southern Arabia was automatically reduced sharply and the land became gradually more isolated.

Many scholars have placed some of the blame for the decline of wealth in southern Arabia, on the collapse of the Marib Dam. The superior culture had depended to a great extent on sophisticated irrigation systems. The largest was the great dam at Marib, located in present-day North Yemen. It was built across Wadi Dhana, constructed of earth and faced with stone and sections of it can be seen today. It was unique because its great length of 600 metres spanned the wadi between two sluices and diverted water from flash floods into a system of canals which irrigated 4,000 acres. It is generally held that its collapse in the sixth century AD was caused by massive silting. Agriculture declined as a result and this had a devastating affect upon prosperity.

Marib was the capital of the Kingdom of Saba (biblical Sheba). This civilization began in the first millennium BC. There were, in fact, five other separate kingdoms in southern Arabia during this period, but they did not prosper simultaneously.

Trade did not cease with the decline of the south – the northern markets still existed and the Hijaz prospered and grew in importance.

In the seventh century AD, Arabia once again rose to eminence when the Prophet Muhammed (570–632 AD) introduced Islam – "submission" to the will of God. As a result of being persecuted for his religious beliefs in his birthplace, Mecca, Muhammed migrated to Medina in 622 AD. The Islamic calendar dates from this migration, known as the *Hejira*. When the Prophet's Heavenly Message had become widely accepted throughout Arabia, he began to propagate it beyond the borders of Arabia.

After the Prophet's death, the leaders of Islam, known as the *Khalifate* (meaning successors), continued to expand the Islamic empire. Islam spread rapidly throughout the Middle east, North Africa and much of southern Asia. The *Khalifate* transferred their capital from Medina to Damascus (in present-day Syria) and later to Baghdad (in what is now Iraq). The Peninsula was then relegated to the status of a province and to relative obscurity, dignified chiefly by its possession of the two holy cities, Mecca and Medina.

The Islamic empire enjoyed a golden age during the period it was ruled from Baghdad. Art, science, philosophy, mathematics, literature and all the creative manual skills developed and flourished. The Crusades – which began in 1096 AD and lasted for 300 years – brought European civilization and culture into contact with this thriving Islamic empire.

The prosperity ended with the Mongol invasion of 1258 AD under Hulagu Khan. Untold thousands were slaughtered, magnificent cities were razed to the ground and enormous areas of fertile land were laid waste. The Mongols' destructive force was felt again between 1393 and 1402 AD under the leadership of the infamous Tamerlane. Thus ended the great Islamic Empire. These events reduced most of the Peninsular people to desperate straits and they suffered still further from frequent internal strife.

The trend in fortune changed for Arabia in this century with the rise of the House of Saud. Abd al-Aziz ibn Abd al-Rahman Al Saud (1880–1953), the son of an *Amir* or Arab Chieftain who had been forced into exile by a rival family, set out at the age of twenty to restore the earlier political dominance of his tribe and to unite the people of the Arabian Peninsula under a single banner.

The prince, Abd al Aziz, became known as Ibn Saud, and his success story, so full of drama and romance, is told world-wide. In 1902, he led a very small band of armed men to surprise and capture Riyadh, the capital of the Najd and the ancestral home of the Saud family. Neighbouring Bedouin tribes, impressed by his valour and success, rallied to his banner. His dream to unite true believers of Islam, despite their tribal affiliations, was to be realized through a combination of military campaigns, marriage alliances and social reforms. Also, Ottoman garrisons began to withdraw from the Peninsula in 1913. Then World War One put an end to the Ottoman empire.

In 1924, Ibn Saud entered Mecca for the first time, wearing the humble garb of a pilgrim; the following year, he reopened the country to other pilgrims, guaranteeing them safe passage to the holy cities. In 1926, he was proclaimed King of the Hijaz and, in 1927, King of the Hijaz and the Najd and its dependencies. Finally, in 1932, he decreed that his united realm, which comprised most of the Peninsula, was to be known as the Kingdom of Saudi Arabia.

The most important event in the recent history of Arabia, thereafter, was the discovery of oil in the 1930s. Oil was found in Bahrain in 1932, Saudi Arabia and Kuwait in 1938, Qatar in 1939, Abu Dhabi in 1960, Oman in 1964, Dubai in 1966 and Sharjah in 1974. The other member countries of the United Arab Emirates (formed in 1972), Ajman, Umm Al-Qaiwain, Ras Al-Khaimah and Fujairah, do not have oil in viable quantities.

Economic development stimulated by the growth of the oil industry has been remarkably rapid. Even nomadic Bedouin in remote regions have now been introduced to Western technology and material culture and have taken the fruits of trade with the West into their tent dwellings.

Throughout their turbulent history, the Bedouin's legendary social courtesy has remained constant. It is paradoxical that the sparsely inhabited and inhospitable deserts should produce a people who exemplify perfect hospitality. Knowledge of this gracious tradition reached the outside world long ago while the land itself remained virtually unknown until this century.

Today, vast oil reserves have provided a new basis for Arabia's wealth. The wheel of fortune has turned full circle and most of the Peninsula thrives once again. Trade with the outside world has brought this fascinating place under the gaze of the curious West. The world has come to realize that the Kingdom of Saudi Arabia, and the other Peninsula countries, are built upon the values of an ancient society and remain strongly committed to these values and the tenets of Islam. It is symbolic of the desire to preserve such values that museums are being established to display all aspects of historic and ethnic interest.

Within the Kingdom of Saudi Arabia, the hub of these museums is situated in Riyadh, the capital. It was the first public museum and opened officially in 1979 under the guidance of the Director of Antiquities and Museums, Dr. Abdullah H. Masry. Much earlier, regulations were drawn up to protect the cultural heritage of Saudi Arabia. These required that weaponry and artifacts of stone and wood should be submitted to one of the special offices established throughout the Kingdom before making plans for export. The Riyadh Museum is one primarily devoted to the display of archaeological discoveries and, at its inception, archaeology was stressed as being of cultural, national and humanistic concern to the Kingdom. As time went on, items of ethnic interest appeared in and about the building. Bedouin jewellery took its place beside a broad range of Arabian art-crafts that are now a permanent display. Awareness of their importance grew until it reached the point where they are now accepted as integral to the full picture of Arabia's history.

13

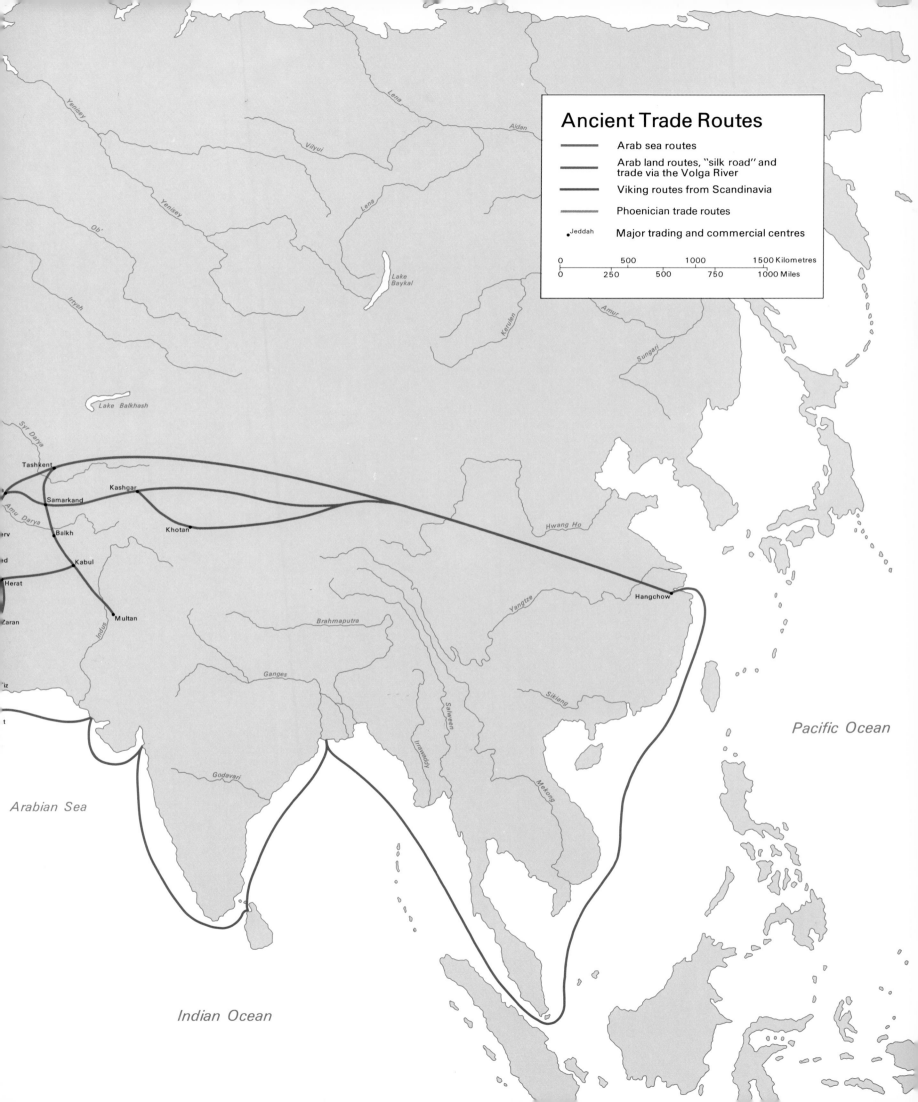

Ancient Trade Routes

Arab sea routes

Arab land routes, "silk road" and trade via the Volga River

Viking routes from Scandinavia

Phoenician trade routes

•Jeddah Major trading and commercial centres

500 1000 1500 Kilometres
0 250 500 750 1000 Miles

Tashkent

Kashgar

Samarkand

Balkh

Khotan

Merv

Kabul

Herat

Multan

Zaran

Hwang Ho

Yangtze

Hangchow

Brahmaputra

Ganges

Godavari

Indus

Salween

Irrawaddy

Mekong

Sikiang

Yenisey

Ob'

Irtysh

Yenisey

Vilyui

Lena

Aldan

Lena

Lake Baykal

Kerulen

Amur

Sungari

Lake Balkhash

Syr Darya

Amu Darya

Pacific Ocean

Arabian Sea

Indian Ocean

Influence

Written records of tributes and gifts taken by north Arabian Bedouin chiefs to Mesopotamian and Assyrian kings reveal that the Arabian Bedouin have worked both gold and silver since ancient times. Further evidence of the long history of body ornament in Arabia was found in a pre-Islamic tomb excavated in Jawan, north of Qatif in the Eastern Province in 1952, and at Faw (south-west central Arabia) in 1979.

Although the Jawan tomb was robbed in antiquity, gold jewellery and beads remained. Accurate dating of the burial was difficult because water had entered the tomb, but artifacts present set the date at about 500 years before Islam. The occupants of the original tomb were apparently members of an important family and their possessions show that they were in contact with India, Parthia and the Romano-Hellenic worlds. No silver ornaments survived, except small pieces of purplish metal which may have been fragments of finger-rings. A purplish discolouration on clay in several parts of the tomb proved to be silver chloride, from which it was deduced that silver head and breast ornaments had been worn. The gold jewellery is elaborate and finely crafted. F. S. Vidal, the archaeologist responsible for the excavation, describes some unstrung beads retrieved from the neck of a body: "The position of the beads indicated that the girl had been wearing a necklace made of a variety of stones: garnet, carnelian, amethyst, onyx and pearls, and a few small gold beads in a variety of shapes: bulbar, annular, cylindrical, mace-shaped and two shaped like cowrie shells".

Although silver jewellery may have been worn as much as gold in the ancient world, all but a few pieces have perished because silver tarnishes when exposed to sulphur compounds in the air and the oxidation process ultimately destroys the metal. Gold, by contrast, is remarkably stable and impervious to the ordinary processes of corrosion and decay; thus ancient gold body ornaments are available for study.

Bedouin silver jewellery is tremendously exciting because its techniques and styles bear striking resemblances to those of civilizations long dead. For example, the traditional mace-shaped terminal bead of today's Bedouin necklaces is identical to that of the Jawan necklace which was dated at about 100 AD, matching also, in both design and period, a Tillya Tepe, northern Afghanistan necklace. Fortunately, the early beads were made of gold and therefore survived to provide this evidence.

A British Museum publication states that "the Islamic world inherited the jewellery techniques and styles of Graeco-Roman Syria and Egypt and of Sassanian Persia, with the earliest examples from Fatimid Egypt and Seljuk Persia" and the decorative styles "developed under the patronage of the Seljuk Turks" wherein "fine silver-gilt and nielloed ornaments were worn". "Islamic" here would seem to refer primarily to jewellery from parts of the Middle East other than the Peninsula, as niello is not part of the Arabian jewellery tradition and gilding is not common to the heartland of the Peninsula. Arabian Beduoin jewellery styles are, in fact, more ancient than Islam, but the ornaments exhibit Islamic innovations. Islamic body ornament, therefore, has another branch which deserves consideration, namely, Arabian Bedouin jewellery.

Most Bedouin ornaments are silver, although a few items such as buttons, beads, rings and forehead pieces are made of gold. Rarely is any of the silver jewellery more than fifty years old, as it is usually melted down after the death of its owner, in accordance with tradition, to be sold as silver or to be reworked into new pieces. Presumably, jewellery is melted down because, as the personal property of a Bedouin wife and given to her as dowry, it would be unacceptable to a new bride. Moreover, it is likely the jewellery would show signs of wear and possibly damage after a lifetime's use.

In the past, Bedouin men often wore heavy jewellery. Islamic prophetic tradition, however, enjoined male Muslims not to wear ornaments made of gold or highly precious stones. Only silver was considered correct. Some have claimed that Islam requires Muslim women to wear only silver ornamentation, but this view has been refuted by learned scholars. Perhaps the beauty of silver appealed more than gold to the Arabian Bedouin of the past, as it does to Scandinavians today; or silver may have been more readily available and, of course, it is less expensive than gold.

Craftsmen still produce traditional Bedouin jewellery throughout Arabia today, but many of them are retiring and the younger generation is turning to more profitable occupations. These facts, combined with the Saudi Arabian Bedouin's current preference for mass-produced gold, account for the disappearance of traditional Bedouin ornaments. The Bedouin have obviously been influenced by what it essentially an urban preference for gold; also, because jewellery – as a portable commodity of nomadic peoples – has always been an ideal form of savings account, the obvious economics of gold versus silver must have become apparent to them.

16

Related Civilizations & their Influence

Although jewellers today can draw upon any or all cultures for designs, it is rare to see modern jewellery that resembles ancient pieces. One can only marvel at Bedouin jewellery for its accurate reproduction of styles spanning thousands of years. Current fads and fashion obviously made no inroads on the Arabian tradition. The purity of expression with which the jewellery is reproduced, despite a new boldness of interpretation, must be attributed partly to a respect for tradition. However, the comparative isolation in which Arabians lived during their 2,000 year economic eclipse would seem to be primarily responsible for the Peninsular artisans retaining ancient jewellery-making techniques and styles. There is no doubt, however, that Bedouin jewellers of times past actively sought inspiration for ornament design, and this has been welded on to that which existed.

Jewellery making techniques and styles of body ornament have been subject to many influences through the ages. From time to time, innovations are introduced from outside the world of the craftsman, either through commerce or through the clash or amalgamation of civilizations. All art forms were enriched in this way and jewellery is no exception.

Egyptian
The Egyptian (*Masri*) influence on Arabian Bedouin jewellery became particularly apparent when Tutankhamen's tomb was opened in 1922 and the jewellery discovered therein was subsequently displayed. The evidence confirmed that Egyptians favoured multiple pendant ornaments and plain or engraved metal surfaces richly decorated with applied filigree and granulation. They made abundant use of turquoise, carnelian, faience and glass, colourful beads, strung or pendant, and multicoloured combinations of stones set on thin sheets of beaten gold – all these features are also characteristic of Bedouin jewellery.

Most ancient Egyptian jewellery had magical significance – so much so that it is almost impossible for scholars to distinguish the amuletic from the purely ornamental. It is especially difficult because the Egyptians took their everyday jewellery with them to the grave. They believed that the green of feldspar and turquoise was the colour of new life, the red of carnelian the colour of lifeblood and the blue of lapis lazuli the colour of the heavens. The cowrie shell and fish shapes gave protection and the scarab shape was the most potent amulet of all. The Bedouin of Arabia share the Egyptian's love of turquoise, a semi-precious stone used in remote antiquity. Egyptian turquoise in the shape of a scarab (the dung beetle revered as the symbol of regeneration) was found in the tombs of the Pharaohs. In Arabian Bedouin jewellery, it appears occasionally as a silver pendant. The coiled snake was also a popular jewellery motif that had amuletic significance. The Peninsular people may have inherited this shape from the Egyptians and developed it into the coiled snake-like silver bracelets worn by the Bedouin today.

It has been deduced that the earliest Egyptian necklaces were simple strands of beads, and later, during the Middle Kingdom period when the art of the Egyptian jeweller reached its zenith, gold working of every description was performed. The New Kingdom saw the use of imitation gems become more common and styles began to vary for broad collar necklaces. After the New Kingdom period ended, Egyptian jewellery for the most part exhibited Hellenic and Roman characteristics. Bedouin ornaments closely resemble the many rings and ear-rings that were made during this era.

Oriental
Several exotic and ornate pieces of jewellery made by the Arabian Peninsula Bedouin look distinctly Oriental (*Sharqi*) and may be the result of influences brought in when the Silk Road was active, or later during the spread of Islam.

Characteristics of Oriental jewellery shared with Arabian Bedouin are the bell shape, the inclusion of tiny objects in hollow jewellery (these rattle in time to a dancer's movements) and a lavish use of relief ornamentation – often used to build up a domed surface in an elaborate manner.

Reminiscent of Bedouin jewellery, Bhutanese and Nepalese jewellery are distinctive in that they favour high-relief ornamentation often set with turquoise. This chunky jewellery is more closely related to that of Tibet than to that of their other neighbour, India. The Tibetans are different from their principal neighbours, the Chinese and the Indians. Much of their jewellery is devotional. The striking effect of Tibetan jewellery is achieved by an interplay of prominent turquoise encrustation, which sometimes forms elaborate patterns along with an abundance of false granulation, pearled wire and coarse beaded borders used for decorative accent. An affinity with Bedouin buttons and beads can be seen clearly in the roughly cut turquoise mounted in high relief.

The Chinese, too, have used turquoise lavishly in their jewellery for thousands of years and their ornamentation of the third and fifth centuries AD also shows granulation in triangular borders, enhanced further by three minute granules (again forming a triangle) – exactly the same granulated pattern used on Arabian jewellery. The art of granulation probably reached the Chinese from the West. The granulated decoration in diamond patterns used in the Arabian Peninsula, at least from the first century AD, suggests the active link between China and Arabia that began when the ancient Arabian trade routes connected up with the Silk Road.

It has been established that the nomadic Scythians and Russians exerted some influence on Chinese jewellery. Characteristic of Scythian ornamentation was the incorporation of stylized animal shapes into jewellery, particularly as terminals to ornaments. However, this fashion is found over a long period of time and a vast geographical area from Europe to China. Some Bedouin bracelets have terminals which may be derived from an amalgmation of Chinese and Scythian styles of ornament.

Indian

Muslims first entered India to spread their religion but later went as conquerors. Muslims gave new impetus to Hindu creative activity and a new vitality was injected into Indian (*Hindi*) arts and crafts. The greatest contribution was in the field of embellishment. While Indians clung to existing shapes, the Muslims added the fish, crescent and star shapes, and previously plain ornaments became ornate. Indian jewellery design thereafter was a blend of Hindu and Muslim styles; ornaments and precious and semi-precious stones were engraved with holy words; and beautifully ornamented amulet cases carried paper bearing Koranic inscriptions.

The first Mughal emperor, Barbur (descendant of Tamerlane), began a dynasty in 1526 which lasted until 1857. The Mughal emperors were not only great patrons of art but were also knowledgeable connoisseurs. While Islam enjoins a certain degree of austerity, Mughal jewellery never failed to dazzle. In the seventeenth century one emperor, Jahangir, wrote in detail of jewels that were given and received as presents in the imperial court. He mentioned a beautiful rosary of "carnelian from Yemen".

The origins of Indian jewellery lie buried in antiquity. Archaeological finds reveal a wealth of ornaments and statuettes wearing ornaments, indicating an unbroken jewellery tradition. Much Indian jewellery was subject to tribal variation which, of course, led to regional differences as it did on the Arabian Peninsula.

The wearing of jewellery still has strong ritual significance in many parts of the sub-continent. It is enjoined on parents to include a certain amount of jewellery in a daughter's dowry – a custom with parallels in traditional Arabia. At the time of her marriage, an Indian woman puts on jewellery which is removed only when she becomes a widow or at he time of her death. It may involve only one piece, and this marriage ornament differs from area to area; Muslims in India wear a nose ring especially at the time of marriage.

Arabs in India have an old expression "to have a ring in one's ear", referring to a time when the wearing of an ear-ring was connected with being a slave. The armlet, in contrast, was considered an insignia of power and was once worn in India as a mark of royalty – as it was in several other parts of the Middle East. It was also the custom for a dying Indian to be divested of all ornaments and after a prescribed number of days, his widow also removed all her dowry ornaments, breaking glass bangles that were considered symbols of her married status. Similar glass bangles were worn by Bedouin women in northern and eastern Arabia, according to noted Arabists who travelled there in the nineteenth and early twentieth centuries, and evidenced by broken pieces found on ancient sites. Of course, glass jewellery breaks readily, but it is possible, too, that an Indian custom was prevalent at one time in these regions.

A great deal of Indian tribal jewellery bears a remarkable similarity to Arabian Bedouin ornaments because contact and the exchange of ideas has linked the people of both lands throughout their history. Long ago, when Phoenician and Arab traders brought goods back and forth across land and sea, west coast Indian jewellery began to reflect strong Arabian influence. Indians left their own land and settled along the coastline of Arabia, accounting for similarities to Indian ornaments seen in Bedouin jewellery worn in the peripheral areas of the Peninsula.

Central Asian

The Samanids (874–999), who suceeded the Abbasid Caliphate in Samarkand and Bukara, became the most important of the early independent Muslim states in the east. Their cities were important trading centres that brought great wealth to Islamic civilization as part of a booming commercial network.

Locked in by a land barren of natural resources, the Samanids amassed wealth from transit tolls and customs dues. They sat at the crossroads when riches from the north, south, east and west passed through. Gems, jewellery and precious metals were part of the treasure that filtered through Central Asia at this time. Although the prosperity of the land declined about the turn of the tenth century, the people of Central Asia maintained their ancient values. Of the traditional jewellery worn in the region today, it is claimed that most styles have been constant through countless generations.

Some pieces of traditional Arabian Bedouin jewellery strongly resemble Turkoman ornaments. Noted for their simplicity, the designs are characterized by an austere appearance enlivened with minor detail such as filigree and granulation. As in the case of Arabian Bedouin jewellery, the decoration confirms the shape of the ornament. Single red stones, usually carnelian, are centrally set and stand out dramatically. Turkoman jewellery, although basically silver, is often gilded. The Turkoman Yomud tribe also adds blue, green and red glass to their gilded silver pieces, but these are not typically Turkoman.

Central Asian (*Asiawi*), Bedouin jewellery is commonly silver and the women weave rugs in order to buy it. When they set out on the pilgrimage to Mecca, some of the jewellery is sold along the way to boost travel funds and these foreign pieces often appear for sale in the Women's *Souq* in Riyadh. Although it is similar to Peninsula pieces, Central Asian jewellery is relatively easy to discern. Foreign pieces appear during the period just after *Haj*; blue stones are sometimes lapis luzuli instead of turquoise and red stones can be garnets.

As discussed previously, Arabian Bedouin jewellery occasionally exhibits design facets reminiscent of Scythian jewellery. The Scythians were warlike nomads who came from Central Asia to settle on the northern shores of the Caspian Sea – Scythia is now southern Russia. They were skilled jewellers and used gold almost exclusively to produce naturalistic designs and vivid representations of animals that are full of movement and life. Alexander's conquests, in the fourth century BC, hellenized Scythian work and spread this style of ornamentation throughout his Empire. No doubt Islam superimposed an austerity culminating in the further stylization of animal-shaped terminals – the results may well be worn in Arabia.

Phoenician

Phoenicians were at one time the greatest seafaring traders of the ancient world. Because they lived on a narrow strip of land locked out by mountains (present-day Lebanon and the coast of Syria) and lacked sufficient fertile land to farm and raise cattle, they became merchants, seamen and skilled craftsmen. These northern Canaanites also became colonists. They were famed for their skill in glass-making and their jewellery-making techniques. Phoenician goldsmiths were widely known and respected for the quality of their work. In the first century BC, the Phoenicians were responsible for carrying the jewellery styles of western Asia through to the Mediterranean.

Although the Phoenicians are often credited with the invention of glass, this medium had been known since the middle of the second millennium BC. According to tradition, however, glass was accidentally discovered when a group of shipwrecked Phoenician sailors lit a fire on a sandy beach. Colourful glass necklaces were a popular Phoenician adornment; their irregular-sized multicoloured, stranded beads – with pendants placed at regular intervals – are very similar in construction to those worn by the Arabian Bedouin.

Phoenician (*Finiqieen*) ornamentation included amuletic motifs derived from Egyptian jewellery, yet the patterns were often so transformed in shape and combinations of shapes that they would not have been recognized even by contemporary Egyptians.

From the eighth to the fourth centuries BC, the Phoenicians came under the dominance of empires situated to the east in Mesopotamia and Elam, until eventually they were defeated by Rome in the third and second centuries BC. During their years of seafaring service to successive masters – Egyptians, Mesopotamians, Persians, Greeks and Romans – the influence of this vigorous race upon the development of jewellery-making skills was profound and far-reaching.

Persian

The Persian (*Ajami*) influence on Arabian Bedouin jewellery is probably the strongest single outside influence of the past, especially in the north, south and east of the Peninsula, for the Persians mixed freely with the pre-Islamic Bedouin Arabs from these areas.

Studies of ancient Persian body ornament are usually based on the Oxus River Treasure found in 1877, the history of which is unfortunately obscure. The hoard, which may represent an accumulation of two or more centuries of booty, was probably hidden about 330 BC, when Alexander the Great's army was advancing on Persia. Records provide enlightening information. According to Greek historians, remarkable quantities of gold were worn by the Persians. They write of bracelets, torques and appliquéd ornaments.

The Phoenicians, who were dominated by the Persians from 539 to 332 BC, had a profound influence upon jewellery crafted at that time. Yet it can be observed that Persian jewellery tends to be technically simpler than Phoenician ornamentation. It is the Persians' lavish use of gold that gives it singular opulence. Persian jewellery also displays characteristics inherited from Mesopotamia and neighbouring Elam, which appear to have been influenced in turn by the Scythians.

The artistic vitality of the Persians continued unabated throughout the rise and fall of subsequent civilizations despite the conquest of their empire by Alexander. The Persian influence on Bedouin jewellery is unmistakable. The piece that is particularly Persian-looking is a multiple-pendant choker of an elegance rarely matched. The elongated pendant beads are trimmed with bells which are also typical of Persian jewellery. The much discussed stylized animal-head bracelet terminals were fashionable in Persia, too, and Arabia may have received the design from this source.

Celtic

Various pieces of Arabian Bedouin jewellery are astonishingly similar to ornaments of the Celts, the ancients of Western Europe – the Gauls and their continental kin.

Celtic (*Celti*) jewellery of the first century BC, found in England and France include the torque, or neck-ring, which is regarded as the principal Celtic piece. There are matching hoop bracelets made from twisted rods. This style was crafted by Bedouin silversmiths in the past for belts, neck-rings and bracelets. Today, only the bracelets can be found for sale, although one collector possesses a belt and others have neck-rings. A similar torque is still worn in Afghanistan, albeit with the addition of a tiny flower motif placed at each side of the neck.

Surprisingly, these wrought hoops are held to be from the Najd and central Arabian in conception. The possible bearer of Celtic influence for this style may have been the seafaring Phoenicians, who carried on a long-established trade between the Middle East and the western Celts. To further their commerce, Phoenicians set up trading posts that later became colonies (the city of Marseilles in what is now France is one such example). They sailed as far as the Baltic Sea and the west coast of Africa trading tin from England, silver from Spain, fur from the Baltic Sea area, gold and ivory from Central Africa, linen and glassware from Egypt and perfumes and spices from Arabia. As jewellers, they may have copied Celtic styles; possibly Celtic jewellery was among their cargo.

Despite the fact that ancient Arabian Bedouin jewellery is rarely found, it is possible to discern evidence of early cultural contact, such as the Celtic – Phoenician – Arabian connection by observing ancient jewellery. Although it is impossible to tell at this point, there is the likelihood that Celts may have taken up an Arabian style of jewellery.

Greek

Early Greek (*Ighriqi*) jewellery, made between 850 and 700 BC, demonstrated the highest standards of workmanship. It is probable the famed Phoenician goldsmiths set up workshops and taught the secrets of their trade to Greek apprentices, because the Greeks had previously suffered two or three centuries of great poverty during which they had produced very little jewellery.

The Greeks eventually became highly skilled jewellers but they used little colour in the form of gemstones. Instead, their craftsmen employed decorative techniques – especially granulation – to embellish plain metal surfaces. Although jewellery found in the Pyramids attests to the Egyptian's use of granulation, it is the early Greeks who are credited with developing it. It is likely the technique reached Arabia from Egypt and any refinement of its use could have come to the Peninsula much later from the Greeks and Etruscans, or perhaps through the Graeco-Roman amalgam of the Byzantine Empire.

The Greeks also favoured filigree. Their application of this decorative technique, and particularly their use of pendant bells on necklaces of the seventh century BC, is parallelled in Bedouin jewellery.

In the Classical Greek period (600 to 475 BC) jewellery again was rare but became more plentiful after the Persian wars. Gems were rarely used, however, and filigree became increasingly popular although the work was not as fine as that done before the Persian wars.

The first engraved stones appeared during this period and the Greeks eventually became the finest gem engravers of the ancient world. Elaborate necklaces were also crafted and, by the end of this period (fifth to fourth centuries BC), Greek jewellers were producing high quality pieces.

The Hellenic Age, which began with the conquests of Alexander, late in the third century BC, transformed the Greek world and the former Persian Empire. Persia was Hellenized by Greek settlement and the Greeks in turn were exposed to the newly conquered Egyptian and western Asian civilizations. The Hellenic age ended with the emergence of the Roman Empire in 27 BC.

During this period, massive finger-rings set with stones wider than a single finger became fashionable – a style seen in Bedouin finger-rings. Among the new jewellery motifs appearing during the Hellenic age was the crescent shape, introduced to Greece originally in the sixth and seventh centuries BC, from western Asia where, as a symbol of the moon god, it had had amuletic significance in remote antiquity.

There are at least two positive links in the historical chain of Arabia's jewellery and these indicate the influence of Greece. The mace-shaped terminal beads retrieved from a tomb (circa 100 AD) at Jawan in the Eastern Province of Arabia are identical in shape to Greek beads of the fourth century BC. The same style of bead occurs in Arabian Bedouin jewellery, albeit fashioned in silver. It is worn in the same position today as the early Greek example.

Roman

It is generally agreed that the Romans were indebted to the Greeks for their jewellery styles. From the beginning of the Roman Empire, in 27 BC, the formerly austere Romans began to wear fabulous jewellery which at first merely imitated Hellenic styles. However, despite the considerable impact of Greek jewellery, the Romans themselves perfected several jewellery-making techniques, such as wire-making. Furthermore, although the Greeks were considered the first and finest gem engravers in the ancient world, the Romans were responsible for engraving gems with many fantastic designs. During the Roman period, great care was taken to ensure that the subject of an engraving corresponded to the colour of the gem engraved. Cows were engraved on green jasper, the slaying of Marsyas was executed on red carnelian, marine deities were cut into aquamarine and harvest scenes usually appeared on gold-coloured gemstones.

Massive finger-rings, popularized by the Greeks, became particularly fashionable with the Romans. Also popular, during this era, were several rings designed to be worn at once, one on each finger. Sometimes the Romans wore several slender rings, each set with a different stone, uniting into one. Roman (*Rumani*) rings invariably exhibited elaborate tapered shoulders that were often carved. All these characteristics and fashions are found in the design and wearing of Bedouin finger-rings in Arabia today.

Betrothal rings first appeared in Roman times and have continued to be a symbol of marriage ever since, although the forms of these rings have varied greatly over the centuries. The plain bands of today, which bear no resemblance to the betrothal rings of the past, appear to have made their appearance in the West as late as the beginning of this century. Plain bands were worn on the "wedding" finger prior to this date, but were known as "keeper" rings, being placed on that finger simply to keep the other ring or rings safely in place. Although the Arabian Bedouin of the past did not have a betrothal ring as such, jewellery given as dowry upon marriage does contain finger-rings. Modern Arabians now follow the tradition of the betrothal ring begun by the ancient Romans.

The snake shape, which had amuletic significance for Egyptians, was worn by the Greeks and continued to be popular with the Romans, a fashion persisting in the jewellery of the Western world. Possibly the snake-like coils that appear as Bedouin bracelets today were derived from Roman ornaments. The snake certainly had symbolic significance very early in the history of the Arabian Gulf area, as is evidenced by the remains of snakes excavated in sacred burials in Bahrain, the site of ancient Dilmun. Geoffrey Bibby, a noted English archaeologist working with a Danish expedition, writes that these snakes, which were generally accompanied by a pearl or blue bead, appeared to be buried beneath the floors of houses of the Dilmun civilization in the belief that they would protect the occupants.

Etruscan
The Etruscans are a race of uncertain origin. They settled in Italy about the ninth century BC, establishing themselves in what is now Tuscany and creating a civilization that flourished in the northern part of the Italian isthmus from about 700 BC. The Etruscans reached the height of their power between the sixth and fifth centuries BC, declined in the fourth century BC until they were eventually absorbed by Rome in the middle of the second century.

Early Etruscan (*Etruwi*) jewellery of the seventh to fifth centuries BC was characterized by its abundance, its technical perfection and its variety. The Etruscans loved colour and used beautiful Phoenician glass and faience in their jewellery to excellent effect. The basics of jewellery-making reached them via the Phoenicians, but they themselves perfected the various techniques and became the most brilliant jewellery craftsmen of this classical age. They were the unrivalled masters of granulation and it is commonly held that their work has never been satisfactorily imitated.

The late Etruscan period (400 to 250 BC) brought forth jewellery fashioned from sheet gold – often convex – and ornamented with simple embossing combined with filigree and granulation. The Arabian Bedouin wear a forehead ornament that echoes these characteristics. Gradually, when the Etruscans were drawn into the Greek cultural orbit, they adopted Hellenic fashions and filigree largely replaced granulation for relief decoration.

The scarab beetle shape was a popular jewellery motif with the Etruscans. They may have adopted it from the seafaring Phoenicians who had in turn taken it from Egypt. Although the Phoenicians considered it merely ornamental, the Etruscans, like the Egyptians, saw it as the symbol of resurrection and immortality. This perhaps provides a clue to their origin.

Byzantine
The amalgamation of the Greek and Roman cultures reached its peak in Byzantia, the eastern Roman Empire. It was there, in the fourth century, that Constantine, the first Roman emperor to be converted to Christianity, established his magnificent new capital on the site of the old Greek town of Byzantium, calling it Constantinople – "Constantine's city". The unprecedented blend of cultures that surrounded succeeding emperors was reflected in their ornaments which combined both pagan and devotional elements.

The Byzantine Empire perpetuated Greek, Roman and Oriental cultures and became the vehicle by which early jewellery-making techniques and styles were borne into the Golden Age of Islam. Greek techniques and styles, superimposed with Roman developments, continued to be subject to change in these early Byzantine and Christian eras. Byzantium became important for its influence on ornamentation styles in other cultures. For the most part, the influence was confined to territories outside Arabia, yet, there are Bedouin ear-rings of definite Byzantine (*Rumi*) derivation – both the pennanular wire hoop style with an attached filigree cage and the crescent-shaped style.

Wire was used extensively in jewellery by the early Christians and Byzantines and a variety of chains and clasps became immensely popular in medieval Europe. Bedouin jewellery also makes much use of chains and the various ornaments have several different types of links with spacers and pendant baubles, combining several crafting techniques. The plainer type of Bedouin chain – a series of simple connections without decorative pretension – illustrates the natural evolution of the earliest use of wire in jewellery. One particular rope-like chain, a type of intricate knitted herring-bone (on the *jnad*), is identical to chains used in early Christian jewellery found in Carthage in North Africa, dated 400 AD. This style of chain also appears in Byzantine jewellery of 600 AD.

The Byzantine Empire thrived for over 1,000 years until Constantinople fell to the Ottoman Empire in 1453, to be renamed Istanbul. Thus, earlier expressions of decorative art flowed into the Ottoman Empire and onward to the rest of the Islamic world.

African

Considering the proximity of Africa to Arabia, the ancient arab trade route connection and the shared Islamic faith that annually brings African Muslims to Mecca on pilgrimage, it is not surprising that Bedouin silver jewellery occasionally exhibits African (*Afriqi*) characteristics. It seems that African craftsmen did not penetrate into the interior of Arabia to settle and therefore the style similarities existing on some traditional Arabian pieces must have been borne along by intermediaries.

The Ashanti, who lived in part of what is now Ghana, fashioned large ornaments of bold design, mostly in gold. Superb gold work was also done in the late fifteenth and sixteenth centuries in Benin, capital of a southern Nigerian kingdom on the western coast, by means of the *cire perdue* (lost wax) process – a technique not used on the Arabian Peninsula. Jewellery from the African continent is fashioned from brass, iron and tin as well as from gold and silver. The similarity to Bedouin jewellery is purely in design.

Establishing when the African influence upon Arabian Bedouin body ornament began is impossible, as cultural contact has been constant through the centuries. It is, in fact, less marked than other influences. Overall, African jewellery is enormous in size, often grotesque and sometimes designed to distort the natural shape of the body.

Beads, of course, are another matter. Arabia for centuries sought beads as jewellery components from other lands including Africa. The most spectacular beads that have found their way to Arabia are cube-shaped amber, which many Africans prized as currency. This amber is not found in Africa and was acquired through trade. It is opaque yellow or orange and claimed as Baltic. There are also many fakes, a fact which confirms the popularity of the style or the production of counterfeit currency.

Although toe-rings are not worn in most parts of Arabia, they are seen in coastal regions in the south – and in neighbouring Africa. This seems to indicate that toe-rings as part of Arabian Bedouin jewellery are an African influence.

Islamic and Crusader

Following the dawn of Islam in the seventh century AD and the subsequent spread of the faith through the former Byzantine Empire, Iraq, Persia, Egypt, North Africa, Spain and east toward China, body ornament in these areas was subject to many influences. It is remarkable that Arabian Bedouin jewellery has emerged so little altered.

The crescent shape (*hilal*) was an ancient prophylactic sign against the Evil Eye. Because of its constant presence, it came into favour as an attractive jewellery shape. It was especially popular with the Byzantines. When this shape was adopted as the symbol of the Ottoman Sultans of Turkey, jewellers throughout the Islamic World were probably encouraged to use it more. Eventually it became the symbol of Islam itself and the crescent is now displayed above mosques throughout the world. It represents the waxing of the moon between new and full moon and ushers in each new month of the *hejiri*, the Islamic year. The crescent remains the most popular motif in Middle Eastern jewellery. Other moon shapes are worn, too – the half (*nasf al qamar*) and the full moon (*badr*). The full moon was romanticized by the great poets of the Classical Age of Islam; according to their verses, a full moon heralds a night for lovers.

The inclusion of religious amulets (*tamimah deeneyyah*), as part of Islamic jewellery, also emanated from the new religion; these often took the form of pendants inscribed with the name of Allah. Other amulets were made up as charm cases containing Koranic verses. A tiny hand usually known as *khamsa*, the Arabic word for five, also had amuletic value in ancient times. Tiny charms supposed to be stylized hands, however, often show three, four or five fingers when they are components of Bedouin jewellery. This inherited shape came to be known as "the hand of Fatimah", referring to the daughter of the Prophet Muhammed. Fatimah was renowned for her great beauty and was said to be one of the few perfect women with whom Allah had deigned to bless the world.

Arabesque, the Islamic form of decoration, also greatly influenced the Bedouin jeweller. In the world of plastic arts, arabesque means a decoration in colour or bas-relief with fancifully entwining leaves and scrollwork – a term originally applied to ornamental Arabic and Moorish architecture. In music it means a work that is conjectured to be decoratively expressive rather than emotionally so. In ballet, a dancer's position and posture denote an arabesque. Arabesque is derived from the Italian word *arabesco* which means Arab. The

Italians were deeply inspired by Oriental themes during the Renaissance and used their designs extensively and as far back as the fifteenth century, they had coined this word and introduced the arabesque style of art to the Western world. Now it is often applied to all forms of art that are richly decorative and consistent in pattern.

Zahi Khuri writes that primitive forms of arabesque existed in pre-Islamic times and were borrowed by the Greeks and Romans, but the richness and most exquisite renderings of this style were achieved by Muslim designers. Essentially it is a linear ornament, an interlaced pattern based on either pure geometric relations with a variety of angular movements or on endlessly flowing curvilinears, sometimes displaying leaf, flower and animal motifs. It is the strength and harmony of their linear designs and their mathematical lucidity that has made them unique and outstanding among other styles of art. It is no accident that Muslim artists adopted this style and developed out of it some of the greatest patterns ever recorded in the history of art.

The simple life in Arabia during the early days of Islam manifested itself in the way Arabs lived in their houses. The only important piece of furniture was the elaborate chest in which clothes and linen were kept. To the Arabs of this early Islamic period, the beauty of the house was expressed by the surfaces that made it – including floor, walls and roof. Much attention was therefore devoted to their decoration. Different motifs, mainly abstract, were developed and utilized to decorate them. The development of arabesques was further encouraged by the early Muslim's aversion to the representation of human beings. Consequently, Muslim calligraphers utilized their talent in copying the Koran and produced the richest of abstract motifs that human imagination can possibly conceive. Since then, Koranic verses and the Kufic script have been blended so magnificently that they have become almost inseparable.

In the eleventh century a major event ocurred that may have affected Middle Eastern jewellery styles. In 1096, prince, peasant and priest marched out of Europe to wage a holy war. This was the first of the series of Crusades – the epic struggle between Christian and Muslim for control of a land held sacred by both. These Crusades, which ended in 1291, were responsible for bringing Western influence to bear upon Middle eastern civilization and culture.

The Crusaders (*Salibiyyun*) are vividly remembered today for their heavy chain mail which may well have influenced the Islamic silversmiths of the period. It is a source of wonderment to see Arabian Bedouin wearing meshed collar necklaces made of interlinking rings, balls and shapes that may have been inspired by this protective garb. It is also interesting to speculate upon the possibility that the Crusaders may have been responsible, to some extent, for increasing the popularity of chains as jewellery.

Modern

In the Hijaz, Western Arabia, lie the holy cities of Mecca and Medina – the goal of Muslim pilgrims from all parts of the Islamic world. Consequently, it is the most cosmopolitan part of Arabia and, as such, has been an important source of foreign influence upon the making and wearing of jewellery. It has also been a main route by which non-Arabian silver ornaments entered the Peninsula in the past. Although most of the Bedouin silver jewellery found in Arabia has been crafted on the Peninsula, occasionally a piece is identified as being from another Middle Eastern country, illustating the mobility of dowry jewellery.

The recent trend in Bedouin body ornament has been toward light-weight mass-produced gold jewellery that is not traditional, although some design characteristics, such as the crescent shape and multiple pendants, have been retained. 18 kt gold jewellery from Italy is bought but 21 kt is preferred. These elaborate, delicate-looking 21 kt gold trinkets that have flooded the jewellery *souqs* were originally imported from India, Pakistan, Syria and Lebanon. Very recently, craftsmen from these countries have begun to work in Arabia to supply the growing demand. Goldsmithing is not new to the Peninsula, however. Lady Anne Blunt and her husband, poet Wilfred Scawen Blunt travelled to Arabia in the 1880s to purchase horses. Lady Anne writes that they found the work of the goldsmiths of Hayil "really good" and "interesting", unlike anything they had seen before. These jewellers were making ornaments, dagger hilts and sheaths.

This preference for modern gold jewellery is clearly not just a matter of gold versus silver, for now Arabian Bedouin women are beginning to appreciate that these ornaments are lighter than the cumbersome traditional styles, especially in the case of nose adornments. Although silver has historically been part of Arabian Bedouin costume, young girls (and many of their mothers) now consider this old-fashioned. Some refuse to wear traditional ornaments, preferring to have a small amount of gold jewellery rather than a large collection of silver. The popularity of gold could be said to symbolize the new affluent phase in Arabia's history, just as the passing of the traditional silver jewellery marks the end of the long era of obscurity.

The Bedouin of the Arabian Peninsula

The Fertile Crescent refers to the segment of land that extends north-westward in a semi-circle from the Arabian Gulf to the Mediterranean. In ancient times, its fertility made it a magnet for wandering Semitic tribes from the arid Arabian deserts and for non-Semitic peoples from the mountainous north. Several remarkable civilizations evolved in this fertile valley including the Sumerian, Babylonian and Chaldean.

The part of the horseshoe that first attracted settlers was the eastern side to the north of the Arabian Gulf between the Tigris and Euphrates Rivers, known to history primarily as Mesopotamia – a Greek name referring to the land between the two rivers. This area today is southern Iraq. In time, the western side along the Mediterranean coast also drew many immigrants.

Not without reason did this area become known as the "Cradle of Civilization", for it gave birth to some of the most important cultural and technical advances of the ancient world. It was a commercial civilization and the first signs of banking appeared in Mesopotamia. Loans were made and interest charged by banker priests who used their temples as financial markets.

Archaeological discoveries within Saudi Arabia suggest a heritage linked with Mesopotamia. It has become apparent that the ancient people of the eastern and northern flanks of Arabia were attracted to this fertile land and it is likely that they contributed to its development. Until these recent revelations occurred, the earliest history of the Arabian people was obscure. Now, Muslim scholars, armed with archaeological evidence, are able to fill in details about their ancestors. Progress is slow, however, due to the nature of the land.

The Arabian Peninsula plateau, that tips slightly towards the east, has a line of rugged mountains in the extreme west, running parallel to the Red Sea coast. The gradual drop eastward toward the Arabian Gulf is broken only by the escarpment of the low Tuwaiq Mountains which extend in a west-facing crescent north and south of Riyadh. Much of the land is covered by sand, forming the three great deserts of the Nafud, the Dahna and the Rub al-Khali. The surface outside the desert is covered by gravel or, in limited areas of the west-central region, by jumbled beds of ancient lava. The climate is hot and dry, with the exception of the south-western and southern highlands where there is sufficient rainfall to support some non-irrigated cultivation. Wadis, the beds of seasonal rivers, mark the course of ancient rivers and lead the rare rains down to the plains. Scattered oases, drawing water from springs and wells, permit some settled agriculture. Humid heat prevails on the coasts.

The first known Arabian civilizations were three coastal settlements. The oldest evidence so far of the presence of civilized man on the Peninsula was found on one of these sites and was identical to those of the Ubaid culture of Mesopotamia. From about 4000 to 2000 BC, the Dilmun civilization dominated the eastern coast of Arabia, extending 60 miles inland to the oasis of Hofuf, including present-day Kuwait and the island of Bahrain. At its zenith, in 2000 BC, Dilmun controlled the route to the east and was the trading link between the

A nomad's life once meant total dependency on camels for transport, and sheep and goats to provide shelter. The tribe was ever on the move in search of pasture and water. An encampment today may have the long, low black Bedouin tents and camels but there is usually a predominance of commercially-made white canvas tents, a water tank and Toyota trucks to be seen.

civilizations of the Indus Valley and those of Mesopotamia. In Oman and Abu Dabi, remains of other civilizations have been found that may well prove to be related to Dilmun also.

Stone structures in northern, north-western and central regions of Arabia, are thought to be associated with early semi-settled populations in these areas. The people who lived there were possibly forebears of the Arabian nomads who were believed to have emerged at a later period in history. It is conjectured that Arabia was only sparsely populated in the interior until about 2000 BC, when migrations from both north and south began. Archaeological evidence indicates that, approximately once every 1,000 years, people migrated from the Peninsula to the more tenable lands around them. As climatic conditions changed and deserts encroached upon arable land, those who remained developed a way of life suited to desert living. This has been maintained to the present day. Also enduring to very recent times was the lifestyle of the settled people living on the periphery of the Peninsula.

The first high culture in southern Arabia is set at approximately 1400 BC. It is believed this was introduced by colonists from the Fertile Crescent. Gus Van Beek, curator of Old World Archaeology at the Smithsonian Institution, writes in *The Rise and Fall of Arabia Felix* that a search for wealth in the developing frankincense and myrrh markets may have been the prime factor in the northern Semites' move to southern Arabia. These Semitic immigrants, he continues, were probably adept at metallurgy when they first settled in the region because, by 1200 BC, the technology of bronze alloying had been known for 1,000 years in the Near East and iron was becoming widely used in the Fertile Crescent. Throughout the first millennium BC, bronze technology was also highly advanced in southern Arabia.

For centuries, the arid and largely desert Peninsula was mainly peopled by nomadic Bedouin (*Badw*). The word "Bedouin" means desert dweller. These hardy and tenacious people – shaped by a harsh environment – raised animals for food and transport as well as for trade. Their existence depended on finding pasture and water for the animals. With such limited arable land, a meagre

Right: *The Antiquities Museum in Riyadh provides an opportunity for visitors to Saudi Arabia to appreciate the atmosphere of tent life. This is a unique experience also for many subjects who have never lived a nomadic life. The colour of tribal ways is fading as fast as the hues in old Bedouin weaving. It is fortunate that so many artifacts are now being collected officially.*

Right: *On the front lawn outside the Museum, a permanent display of Bedouin riding gear, weapons, cooking utensils and items suited to the general desert lifestyle can be enjoyed by Arabs who often feel nostalgic about their past. Many wealthy and successful businessmen take every opportunity to escape their heavy commitments and spend evenings in the desert.*

Right: *Camel accoutrements are very colourful indeed. Tribal women were once adept at producing distinctive patterns for their personal litter and to enhance the family's horses and camels. The display at the Riyadh Museum provides an Arabian lady today with the only opportunity to see this aspect of her cultural heritage. Many families have been town dwellers for centuries, but, not so very long ago, a camel train with all its romantic mystery was a common sight for all to see as it approached each town bearing necessities and luxuries.*

rainfall and a lack of sufficient permanent water, their search was unrelenting. They spent the hottest months of the year in the vicinity of the widely separated oases or in the uplands, moving to the plateau in search of grass in late winter and spring. The rare, brief Arabian rainfall can transform a section of desert by germinating long dormant seeds into vegetation and some of these species can survive for several years without further rain. The great sand deserts are totally waterless and have always been uninhabited, except for wandering Bedouin tribes searching for pasture.

Bedouin savings are traditionally invested in

Courtesy of Antiquities Museum, Riyadh

additional livestock and silver jewellery. The jewellery is sometimes used in commercial dealings in a desert town *souq*, the central market place which is a gathering spot for settled inhabitants and visiting Bedouin alike. Customarily, the *souq* is the temporary camping ground for Bedouin trading their livestock for coffee, tea, rice and other needs. In isolated rural areas, the *souq* usually gathers only once a week – on different days so they can be attended in succession by the traders. Despite the introduction of money, barter in the *souqs* is still common.

Although nomads perpetuate jewellery styles by seeking traditional pieces, they do not make the ornaments. It is generally the settled desert dwellers, concentrated at oases and coastal towns, who make jewellery and handicrafts. The traditional industries include spinning, dyeing, weaving, sewing, embroidery, palm-frond weaving, pottery-making, leather-work, wood-work and metal-work. The latter craft employs gold, silver and base metals for jewellery, sheathed daggers and cooking utensils. These products are seldom exported. Export industries include leather tanning, food processing, date packing and soap making which are also supplied for local consumption. Maritime industries once included pearl-fishing and coral gathering. All Arabian industries, particularly handicrafts, have yet to recover from a general decline in the 1950s, caused by the impor-

tation of cheap manufactured items and the loss of labour to the oilfields.

When the Bedouin barters for his needs, time is of little consideration and the personal exchange between buyer and seller is highly ritualized. Great satisfaction is derived from the bargaining process, which provides an opportunity for those involved to demonstrate their skill in concluding transactions while exchanging gossip and opinions at the same time. After a number of proposals and counter-proposals, agreement on a price is reached. A clever bargainer gains both social prestige and gratification if he believes he has made a good transaction. The shop-keeper is usually happy because he allowed for some reduction in price.

Traditionally, in the desert regions, kinship was the primary organizing principle. The patrilineal extended family, composed of related lineages tracing descent from a common ancestor, formed the basic social and economic unit. Each family constituted a relatively independent group; some large groups had thousands of members and other small ones consisted of only a few lineages. In most tribes, the claim of common descent can no longer be substantiated, but, in a few important cases, the genealogies are carefully preserved. Each lineage is headed by a *sheikh*, who makes decisions framed by the consensus of the male family heads within the group. The *sheikh* is usually one of a particular family in which the right to provide leadership is inherited. A tribal *sheikh* holds *majlis*, a gathering where he listens to requests, complaints and opinions put forward by senior members of his tribe.

The most cohesive tribes in Arabia are found among the nomadic Bedouin, where each unit usually herds the animals owned by its constituent, extended families in a certain territory, or *dirah*. In the past, they banded together with other tribes only in response to particular political or economic conditions. For example, in times of war, large numbers of tribesmen would gather under a particular leader, or, in summer, hundreds of tents from one or more tribes might congregate by a large well or oasis.

The Bedouin's social structure and mode of living, imbued with the ancient values and simplicity, changed little over the centuries. Then, in 1932, following the unification of the country by Ibn Saud, a spirit of wider brotherhood was engendered. Although the tribes had always shared a common heritage and a strong belief in Islam, this new allegiance gave them a sense of nationhood for the first time. The Bedouin are intensely conscious of their Islamic heritage and feel a strong loyalty to their king as the *Imam*, leader of the faithful and protector of the shrines of Islam.

The Arabian Bedouin's tribal structure has been weakened in recent years as a result of the development of the oil industry and the gradual settlement of both nomads and semi-nomads in villages and cities. Yet, whether nomadic or settled, the Arabian characteristic and legendary courtesy, rooted so deeply in the customs and traditions of centuries, remains constant. Customs, too, are generally maintained.

Left: The beads in this necklace were found loose about the neck of a young girl who was buried in pre-Islamic times in a Seleucid tomb complex at Jawan, ten kilometres south-west of Ras Tanura in the Eastern Province of the Kingdom of Saudia Arabia. The circular pendant was close by. It is likely that this necklace has been incorrectly re-threaded as necklaces of that period and earlier were threaded in the same fashion as they are by the Arabian Bedouin today. The mace-shaped beads would be placed in terminal position connected to the clasp or tie, and the pendant would be worn in the centre. All other beads would have the matching sizes spaced at regular intervals – a graduated strand such as this is most unlikely.

Right: This special map has been devised to assist the reader comprehend the tribal locations of long ago in relation to the topography of the Arabian Peninsula. The three deserts, from north to south, are the Nafud, the Dahna, and the Rub al Khali, or Empty Quarter. The modern designation for the Najd (central region) and the Asir (south-western region) have been drawn but no northern border has been included for the Hijaz, northern region, or Eastern Province because tribal grounds extend beyond the present-day limits. The eastern section groups the Arabian Gulf lands. The southern section takes in all those lands which seem logically grouped for study purposes. There are, of course, body ornament differences within each of these broad definitions and these are mentioned.

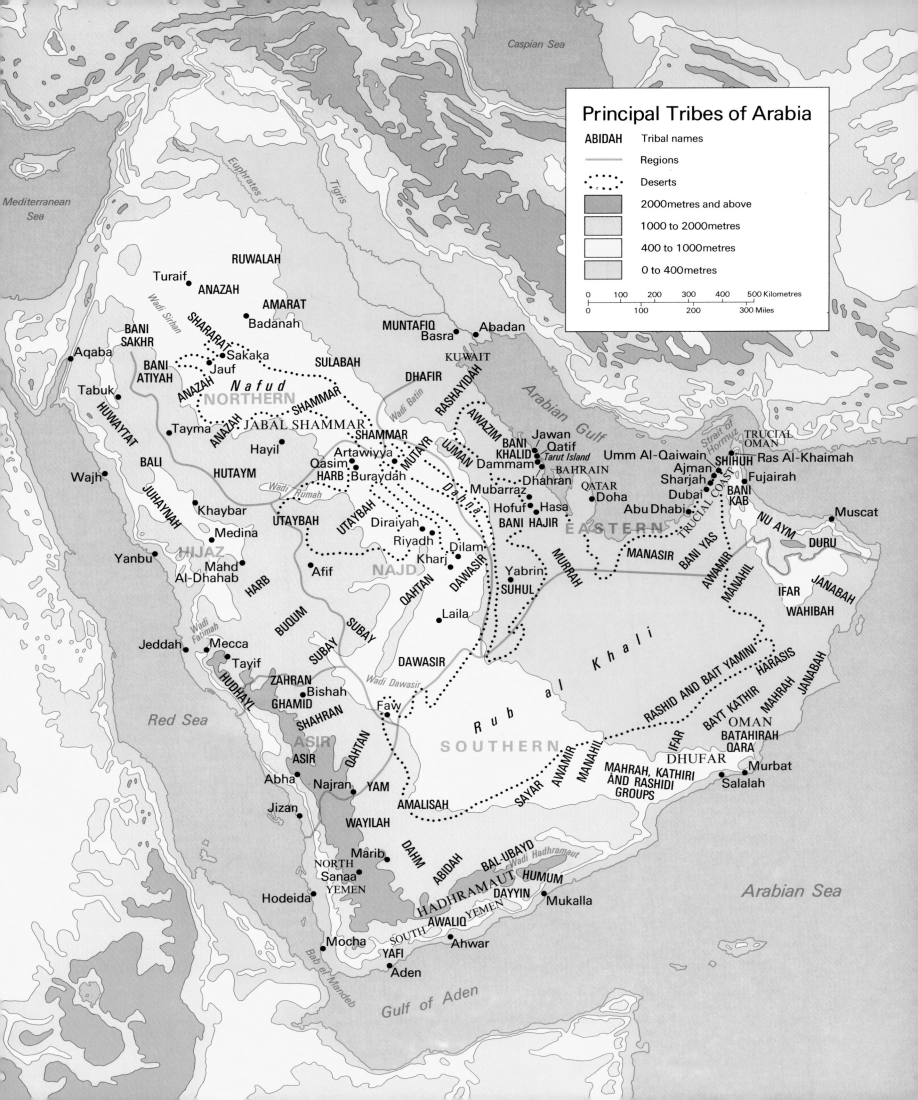

Dowry, known as *mahr* in Arabic, is a strong tradition among the Bedouin, although the form that dowry takes varies greatly and is often paid in kind rather than cash. It has been known to be represented by a piece of jewellery. The *mahr* is generally divided into two sums: the *muqaddam*, or first part, is paid at the time of engagement and the

is equally unlikely he would spend frivolously any portion that he might manage to save. The fact that he buys his daughter silver jewellery as part of her dowry puts the importance of these ornaments in clear perspective.

The marriage is regarded as a civil contract, *milak*, and this is drawn up by the fathers of the

muakhkhar, or second part, is a sum promised to the wife in case of divorce.

Traditional Bedouin marriages are generally arranged within the kinship group by the parents on behalf of the young people. The prospective husband (*arease*), makes his bridal payment to the girl's father (*aab*), before the marriage is consummated, as it is customary for the bride's father to use some of this payment to purchase clothing for the bride (*arousah*), articles for her new home, livestock and jewellery as an investment for her future security.

The father of the bride may go to a settled artisan in a nearby town to purchase the quantity of hand-made jewellery required as an acceptable percentage of the *mahr*, or he may buy it from an itinerant trader or silversmith. It may be purchased within his own tribe, as some of the larger tribes employ their own silversmith to supply needs. Whatever the source, the quantity of items purchased and the workmanship might be similar to those bought by a neighbour. The sum invested could be more or less, however, depending on the silver content. Silversmiths commonly produce varying qualities to suit all pockets.

It is conceivable that a Bedouin would rarely accumulate great wealth with his way of life and it

Above: A woven goat's hair and sheep's wool tent is a cozy and practical home in the desert. The nomadic women weave the tent strips and sew them together. The back section and dividing curtains are usually striped and this colourful work displays tribal patterns. Most of a woman's day is spent within the home where women and girls take care of the children and prepare meals. In the past, they hand-sewed clothing for the immediate family from home-spun, hand-dyed and woven textiles. These were usually embroidered. Leisure time is spent entertaining the womenfolk from other tents or visiting them to exchange news and plan the next social occasion. This may be a wedding for which they will joyfully sew colourful new clothes.

bride and groom before a tribal *sheikh* – a respected member of the tribe. There are also two witnesses as this occasion is considered more important than the wedding night *duklah* or celebration, *farah*. At this time, the bridegroom offers the *mahr* as his pledge of good faith; the silver jewellery under Muslim law becomes the bride's personal wealth. The Bedouin bride accepts this tribute as her right according to custom and tradition. Her jewellery proclaims her new status as a married woman of property. As it is entirely her own, she has the right to sell it if she so desires. There must be an element of security engendered by this wise custom. Less practical but no less important is the fact that a Bedouin woman, like any other, prizes her jewellery for its prestigious and decorative roles.

Alois Musil, who travelled in Arabia early this century, provides an interesting sidelight on the acquisition of jewellery among the far northern Bedouin. According to Musil, women of the Rwalla tribe often saved up camel hair or set aside grain in order to finance the purchase of jewellery for themselves. This practice of women buying their own jewellery is common further north amongst Bedouin in regions such as Afghanistan. Such women weave rugs in order to buy silver

jewellery.

The bulk of a Bedouin woman's jewellery comes to her at the time of marriage. It is considered desirable for a girl to marry before her sixteenth birthday; a boy usually marries between the ages of sixteen and eighteen. Physical beauty and a pleasant disposition are sought in a bride. Family prestige is also considered, as a satisfactory social status and adequate material circumstances are regarded as essential foundations for a successful marriage. It is believed that affection should grow out of a marriage, not precede it. It is also most important that the bride should be a virgin before marriage and a faithful wife afterwards; otherwise disgrace and dishonour fall upon her family.

The eventual marriage celebration, generally held in the evening, frequently occurs in two stages, one at the home of the girl's family where the couple usually live for some days and one at

Above: Hospitality made the desert less vast, less arid and less lonely. A traveller could be sure of a welcome after days of solitary travel across seemingly endless stretches of barren terrain. The Bedouin are hardy people and well-disciplined. A man existed on a little food and water – his camel on less.

the bridegroom's dwelling where the couple will eventually live. Occasionally, the newlyweds will live apart from the bridegroom's family but close by. For the girl's family, the occasion is one of mingled sadness and excitement as she is leaving them to join another family, although she is bringing honour to her own family by taking her place as a member of the community. During the ceremony, the bride is seated in an elevated place so that her bridal clothes, jewellery and appearance may be observed and applauded by all present. A poor Bedouin girl may receive very little jewellery on the occasion of her wedding but, if her family can arrange it, she will wear borrowed jewellery so that she can be presented in the customary splendour.

Music, dancing and singing, as well as refreshments are part of the celebration at the bride's home. Sometimes an animal is slaughtered and a banquet provided. When the time comes for the bride to leave her mother's home, friends and relatives of the bridegroom usually come to escort the bride to her new home where there is more feasting and gaiety. Traditionally men and women celebrate separately.

Although marriages are normally entered into with the expectation that they will last for the lifetime of the partners, it is not required that they be preserved under all circumtances. In Islam, there is no disgrace in divorce and many adults have two or three marriages in their lifetime. Most unions are monogamous, but some men do have two or more wives at one time; a man is allowed

Right: *No so many years ago, it was possible to buy from a broad selection of Bedouin jewellery. This style of forehead ornament, or* kaffat, *might be 24 kt. gold or brass and the stones would be turquoise with semi-precious red stones or glass. Usually the pendants were genuine Gulf pearls but sometimes beads sufficed. They are still available but a good piece is a lucky find and the price is high.*

four wives under Islamic law as long as he observes the Koranic injuction that he treat them equally. If a man takes more than one wife, he is generally expected to maintain each in separate quarters. Sometimes, however, a second wife is brought into the household of the first wife and they get along well together. In this case, they share household tasks and responsibilities.

Relations between a Bedouin husband and wife are characterized by respect and consideration. Although the husband nominally makes decisions for the family, including marriage arrangements,

Above: *Basins of tangled traditional silver and bowls of modern reject pearls greet the eager-eyed customer at the Women's* Souq *in Riyadh. The old silver bracelets, armlets and anklets are often parted from their pairs and pendant bells tend to come adrift because of the constant handling by rummaging enthusiasts.*

he generally does so after discussions with his wife. Activities within the home, however, are under the authority of the wife. She is responsible for children and daughters-in-law, and to some extent, for the men themselves when matters relate to the organization of household routines. For all practical purposes a women's activities are confined to the home, but, should she go out in public, she is usually chaperoned by a servant or male member of the family. Women do leave the home sometimes without a servant or male escort. In these cases a group of ladies accompany each other to visit other women or to go shopping.

Large families are desired by the Bedouin as children are regarded as bringing a blessing on the home. A common felicitation is "May you have many children". Special value is placed on sons among the Bedouin, for they will add to the reputation of the family, whereas daughters will "build someone else's house".

The marriage itself obviously confirms the maturity of the individuals involved, yet the partners are traditionally regarded as "complete" adults only upon the birth of a son. Symbolic acknowledgement of the importance of this event is signified by a change in the name by which the

Below: A tray of Bedouin finger-rings and charms in silver and gold, set with pearls, turquoise and red stones, is offered for sale in the Women's Souq in Riyadh. Most pieces are old and display well-worn jewellery-making techniques and a smooth patina. Tribal women are quite happy to sell their old traditional finger-rings for a generous price, and these are replaced with modern gold workmanship.

coped with the widowed and orphaned, the aged and ill, the handicapped and divorced and the problems of the needy. All of these unfortunates are cared for by more fortunate members of the family. Anyone in need of economic aid or protection is expected to turn to his kinsmen. The emergence of Islam in the seventh century did not alter fundamentally the traditional pattern but rather superimposed a concept of broader responsibility. As Muslims accept inequalities of talent and wealth as being ordained by God, they believe that the richer and more fortunate members of the community have a moral obligation to assist and support the poor.

woman was known. Among friends and relatives, the mother may be addressed thereafter as the mother of so-and-so, using the first name of the son.

As soon as they are able, Bedouin children help with the work of the household. The girls are also expected to care for their younger brothers and sisters. After the age of eight or thereabouts, boys are more in the company of their fathers, whereas girls stay with other females. Young people of both sexes are expected to look after their elders.

The extended family system has traditionally

Above left: In a city souq, a blaze of new gold jewellery assaults the eye as one turns a corner into an electrically-lit corridor of shops. This machine-made 21 kt. gold is often set with fake gems and real and synthetic pink corundum, sold as "ruby". Mass-produced pieces come from India, Pakistan, Lebanon, Syria and local workshops.

In the typical nomadic household, the day begins with the first prayer just before dawn. Then, after a light breakfast, the day's activities start. Girls and women take care of household work and meal preparation; boys and men work outside. Care of the family's camels is of vital importance and Bedouin often become very fond of particular animals. Women's tasks include the spinning of domestic sheep's wool and goat's and camel's hair. The yarn is sometimes sold to settled folk to be woven. Nomadic women weave also, producing beautiful *kilim* rugs, camel bags and tent strips. Nomadic tribesmen sometimes do leather-work for their own needs, but, as a general rule, crafts are performed by the sedentary artisan class.

The nomad's diet consists mainly of milk and milk products obtained from their goats, sheep and camels. They also eat dates and rice bought in town markets. The nomadic Bedouin have wheat less frequently. Milk is drunk fresh, or curdled into yoghourt or cheese. Coffee and tea are the favourite beverages. Meat is eaten only on special occasions when an animal is slaughtered or when wild game is available. They have the opportunity to eat fresh fruit and vegetables when visiting an oasis centre where they barter with the settled cultivators. Despite this meagre diet, the Bedouin are noted for having considerable physical endurance.

The largest meal of the day is served in the evening, as Bedouin men do not usually return home at midday. This meal is a family affair unless there are guests present who are not close relatives. In such a case, the men are served apart from the women and children. Before the meal, there is a long social time. Food is served quite late and friends depart shortly after eating. Women who have leisure time spend it visiting their friends, but, regardless of how they spend the late afternoon, wives are expected to be home to greet their husbands when they return.

Poetry, formal prose and oratory have long been esteemed the highest of the arts in Arabia and they have a special attraction for the Bedouin because his life is essentially spartan. The skilful use of language is a valued accomplishment. A Bedouin poet in the olden days was regarded as the possessor of remarkable powers, the repository of tribal history and guide and spokesman for his tribe. Much of the poetry contains genealogies and tribal histories. The poet was often a warrior himself and he would strive to express in his work the ideals of manliness – gallantry, bravery, loyalty, independence of spirit and generosity. Arabian oral folklore comprises proverbs and stories. The narratives of professional storytellers, whose recitations are particularly in demand during the Muslim month of fasting, *Ramadan*, are very popular in both town and country. These stories provide and perpetuate a wealth of pious, earthy or epic oral tales that have been passed on for generations.

Vocal and instrumental music is also popular as part of the poetic tradition. Musical expression on an informal folk level comprises repetitive bars and intricate beats sometimes played with a coffee-grinding mortar and pestle. The most famous musical instrument is the *oud*, which is similar to a guitar. It is the standard Arabic musical instrument belonging to the family of short lutes and is primarily for solo instrumental music or to accompany a singer. The *oud* is sometimes part of a group at a concert in a semi-settled area. The one-stringed fiddle, *rabaaba*, is also popular and is commonly accompanied by a flute, *nay*, a fiddle, *jozay*, a zither-like *ganoun*, a long lute *buzuk*, a tambourine, *daff*, and a goblet-shaped drum, the *darabukkah*. The ability to improvise a melody constitutes one of the standards by which a performer is judged.

Although dancing is associated with these folk arts, it is not usually a group activity. One of the few exceptions is the Bedouin sword dance, which is performed by men on special occasions. Other exceptional circumstances that provide an opportunity for group dancing within the tribe occur on such festive occasions as weddings, circumcisions and religious holidays – the *Eid al Adha*, or Feast of the Sacrifice and the *Eid al Fitr*, held at the end of Ramadan. Women frequently dance among themselves, but again, they usually perform separately or in pairs.

Above: *In traditional Arabia a Bedouin woman wore her wealth of silver jewellery on every festive occasion. Most of the ornaments came to her as dowry, and she had the right to keep or sell it whenever she chose. This wise custom gave her a feeling of security, and the jewellery lent her prestige among other women.*

Glossary of Arabic Words

Note: No attempt has been made to standardize the transliterated colloquial Arabic words used for the pieces of jewellery. Instead, individual authors have been credited with their own spelling while other words have been recorded as received. There are often several names for an item and variations can occur even within a given region. Yet, words can be remarkably similar over long distances which is most interesting. For example, a necklace can be known as *iqd* (plural: *iqud*) at one end of the Peninsula, and *okd* (plural: *okud*) at the other. Apart from the use of ''K'' instead of ''Q'', it can be seen that only the dialect is different. A waistbelt is generally written *hizam*, but in one case Dickson records a special gold belt, *hazzam*. Both are included. Another type of ornament, the *jnad* in Central Arabia, is described by Ruth Hawley as worn in Oman where it is known as *manjad*.

أب
والـد
Aab
Father

عباية
الحجاب التقليدي الذي تلبسه المرأة
Abaaya
Cloak, mantle, wrapper worn by women

أفريقي
مواطن من قارة أفريقيا
Afriqi
African

أحجار حمراء
أحجار حمراء (مثل الجواهر)
Ahjar hamra
Red stones (as gems)

عين النمر
خرزة تشبه عين النمر
Ain nimr
Tiger eye bead

عجمي
فارسي
Ajami
Persian

عمل سلسلة
صناعة السلسلة
Amal silsilah
Chainmaking technique

أمير
أمير أو زعيم إقليمي أو شيخ قبيله
Amir
Prince or tribal or regional chieftan

عنبر
عمبر
Anbar
Amber

عقيق
حجر كريم
Aqiq
Agate

عقيق أحمر
حجر شبه نفيس،كارنيليان أو جارنت
Aqiq ahmar
Semi-precious stone, refers to carnelian and garnet

عريس
الرجل في ليلة زواجه
Arease
Bridegroom

عروسه
الفتاه في ليلة زواجها
Arousah
Bride

آسيوي
مواطن من قارة آسيا
Asiawi
Asian

بدوي
ساكن البادية
Badawi
Bedouin (adjective)

بـدر
القمر عند كماله
Badr
Full moon

Badw بدو
Bedouin (*Badawi*: male *Badawiya*: female)
سكان البادية

Banagiri بناجيرى
Bracelets, Oman (Hawley)
أساور في عمان

Bangar (Pl. banager) بنجار
Bracelet
سوار ، الجمع : بناجر

Bezr بذر
Seed, referring to seed baroque pearl
حبات اللؤلؤ

Bint بنت
Unmarried girl
فتاة

Boukhor بخور
Frankincense (aromatic resin from the tree *Boswellia carterii*) was the major incense for burnt offerings and funeral pyres in ancient times
مادة صمغية من الأشجار تعطي رائحة جميلة عند حرقها

Burga برقع
Stiff mask worn by women
قناع تلبسه النساء

Buruz بروز
Repoussé technique
شئ نافر أو بارز

Butham بثام
Syn. with *marami*. See *marami*
أنظر مرامي

Buzouk بزق
Long lute
آلة نفخ موسيقية طويلة

Celti سلتي
Celtic
منسوب الى السلتيين أو الى لغتهم

Daff دف
Tambourine
الرق

Darabukkah دربكة
Goblet-shaped drum
طبلة

Dalag دلاج
Mixed bead bracelet (Dickson)
سوار من خرز مختلف

Dara'ah دارة
Full length dress with long fitted sleeves worn by women
قفطان طويل ضيق الأكمام تلبسه النساء

Dhahab دهب
Gold
ذهب

Dhul Hijjah ذو الحجة
Twelfth month of the Islamic calendar, the *Hejiri*
الشهر الثاني عشر من التقويم الاسلامي الهجري

Dirah (pl. diyarat) ديرة
Area or traditional grazing area for a nomadic tribe
منطقة ، منطقة رعي للقبيلة البدوية

Duklah دخلة
Wedding night
ليلة الزفاف

Eid al Adha عيد الأضحى
Feast of Sacrifice beginning on the tenth day of *Dhul Hijjah*
عيد التضحية يبدأ في اليوم العاشر من ذو الحجة

Eid al Fitr عيد الفطر
Feast held at the end of *Ramadan*. The festival of the breaking of the fast occurring on the first of *Shawwal*, commencing with the sighting of the new moon.

عيد يبدأ بعد نهاية شهر رمضان ، الاحتفال بانهاء الصوم ، في بداية شهر شوال ويبدأ عند ظهور القمر

Etruwi إتروي
Etruscan

إتروري ، منسوب الى اتروريا وهي بلاد قديمة في غرب إيطاليا

Fairuz فيروز
Turquoise

تركواز

Farah فرح
The happy event. A Muslim public wedding celebration sealing a marriage in the eyes of God and the community

الحدث السعيد ، الاحتفال بالزفاف الاسلامي وعقد الاتفاق امام الله والاهل

Fatha فص
Finger-ring Rwalla (Musil)

خاتم الاصبع

Fatkah (pl. fatakh) فتكه
Red stone (as gem)

حجر أحمر ، الجمع : فتاكه

Fawariz فواريز
Real and fake turquoise set finger-rings

خواتم للاصبع من التراكواز الحقيقي أو المزيف

Fiddah فضة
Silver

معدن الفضة

Finiqieen الفينيقيين
Phoenician

سكان فينيقية القديمة

Fraida فريضة
Large nose ornament (Dickson)

خزام للأنف

Gadeed جديد
New or modern

شيء جديد

Ganoun قانون
Zither-like musical instrument

آلة موسيقية

Garaz (pl. garasat) جرس
Bell

الجرس

Gub-gub جب جب
Gold cap consisting of linked squares studded with turquoise (Dickson)

مربعات من الذهب تستعمل حلية للرأس في المناسبات

Habbiyat حبيات
Granulation technique

عملية وضع الحبات

Hadith حديث
Sayings of the Prophet Muhammed

أقوال النبي محمد صلى الله عليه وسلم

Hafr حفر
Engraving technique

فن قطع النماذج

Hais Masbukat حيس مسبكة
Syn. with *marami*. See *marami*

انظر مرامي

Haisa حيسه
Finger-ring with coloured stone or a pyramid of mulberry style silver work worn on the fourth finger in Oman (Hawley)

خاتم للإصبع الرابع ، في عمان

Haj حــج
The fifth of the five tenets of Islam, the pilgrimage to Mecca

أداء فريضة الحج ، أحد فرائض الاسلام الخمسة

حجل
خلخال

Hajala
Bracelets, Oman (Hawley)

حجر
الجمع أحجار (أحجار كريمه)

Hajar (pl. **ahjar**)
Stone (as gem)

حلق
حلق للأذن

Halaq
Ear-ring (Dickson)

هامه
إطار من الذهب تتدلى منه سلاسل تعرف بإسم طلال تلبسه العروسة

Hama (pl. **hamat**)
Gold cap with pendant chains, *tallal*, worn by brides (Dickson)

حزام
انظر حزام

Hazzam
See *hizam*

هيكل
تعويذه فضيه كبيره ، في اليمن

Heikal
Large silver cylindrical charm case bead, Yemen (Kennedy)

هجرة
هجرة النبي محمد صلى الله عليه وسلم

Hejira
Migration of the Prophet Muhammed

هجري
التاريخ الهجري ويبدأ بتاريخ هجرة النبي محمد عليه الصلاة والسلام من مكة المكرمة الى المدينة المنورة في عام ٦٢٢م

Hejiri
The Islamic calendar which dates from the time of the Prophet Muhammed's migration to Medina from Mecca in 622 AD, derived from *Hejira*

حاجول
خواتم أصابع من الزجاج أو النحاس

Hgul
Glass or copper finger-rings, Rwalla (Musil)

حجاب
قطعة معدنية تستعمل تعويذة ، أحياناً تكون على هيئة مثلث

Hijab (pl. **ahjibah**)
Charm case, small metal charm or amuletic motif such as a triangle or diamond shape composed of double triangles

حجل
خلخال

Hijl (pl. **hujul**)
Anklet (*hijjil* pl. *hijjal*. Massive gold or silver anklet [Dickson])

هلال
القمر في بداية الشهر العربي

Hilal
Crescent moon

حلية شعر
حلية لتزيين الشعر

Hilyat shaar
Hair ornaments

هندي
مواطن من الهند

Hindi
Indian

حرز
محفظة الحجاب ، أو ورقة عليها آيات قرآنية توضع في الحجاب

Hirz
Amulet charm case or piece of paper on which a Koranic inscription is written, to be contained in a charm case

حزام
حزام للوسط

Hizam (pl. **Ahzimah**)
Waistbelt (*Hazzam*: gold waistband [Dickson])

إغريقي
يوناني

Ighriqi
Greek

علاقة
حلية لغطاء الرأس

Ilagah
Decorative pendants suspended from headgear

إمام
من يؤم المسلمين في الصلاة

Imam
Islamic religious leader in prayer

عقد
سوار لتزيين الرقبة

Iqd (pl. **iqud**)
Necklace

36

عقد مرجان
سوار من المرجان
Iqd mirjan
Ceremonial necklace, Yemen (Kennedy)

عصابة
رباط للرأس
Isaaba (pl. asayib)
Head circlet

إسلام
دين المسلمين
Islam
The Muslim religion, submission to the will of God

إسلامي
متعلق بالدين الاسلامي
Islami
Islamic

جوهرة
حجر نفيس
Jauharah
Gemstone

جوز
خرز من الفضه ، في اليمن
Jauz
Spherical silver bead, Yemen (Kennedy)

جناد
اسورة كبيرة تلبس في الذراع
Jnad
Large necklace worn under one arm

جواهر
مجوهرات
Jowaher
Jewellery

جوزاي
كمان
Jozay
Fiddle

كف
قفاز
Kaff
Glove or ornament composed of one ring for each finger linked to a bracelet by chains and including a decorative piece worn on the back of the hand

كفات أو خمسيات
أشياء لتزيين الجبهة
Kaffat
Syn. with *khamasiyat*. Forehead ornament

كهرمان
عمبر
Kahraman
Amber

خليفة
حاكم اسلامي يحكم بالقرآن والسنة
Khalifa (caliph)
Islamic governor with the role of governing according to the *Koran* and *Hadith*

الخلافة
نظام الحكم في الاسلام
Khalifate (caliphate)
System of Islamic government

خمسيات
انظر كفات
Khamasiyat
Syn. with *kaffat*. See *kaffat*

خمسة
العدد ٥
Khamsa
The number five, also small charm in the shape of a hand

خمزر
خاتم يلبس في الاصبع الصغير
Khamzar
Ring worn on the little finger (Dickson)

خرز
حبات صغيرة
Kharaz (pl. kharzah)
Bead

خرز الحليب
أحجار بيضاء (من الاحجار الكريمة)
Kharaz al halib
White stones (as gems)

خرز الأخضر أو خرز الكبسة
أحجار خضراء (من الأحجار الكريمة)
Kharaz al kabseh or **kharaz al akhdar**
Green stones (as gems)

خاشيل
عقد من العملة الذهبية
Khashil
Necklace of gold coins, known as *sankh* in Kuwait (Dickson)

37

خصير **Khasir**
سوار من حبات العمبر Amber bead bracelets (Dickson)

خاتم **Khatim (pl. khawatim)**
خاتم للاصبع Ring (finger-ring or toe-ring)

خاتم أبو فوز **Khatim abu fauz**
خاتم يلبس في الإصبع الثاني ، في عمان Finger-ring with convex bezel worn on second
finger, Oman (Hawley)

خاتم أبو سيت مرابه **Khatim abu saith mrabba**
خاتم يلبس في الإصبع الثالث ، في عمان Finger-ring with square bezel worn on third finger,
Oman (Hawley)

خزف **Khazaf**
فخار ، صيني Pottery, china, ceramic, porcelain

خزف مزخرف **Khazaf muzakhraf**
صيني ، إناء من الصيني به نقوش Faience

خزامه **Khazama**
حلق لتزيين الأنف يوجد به لؤلؤتين وفصين تركواز Small nose ornament or gold nose-rings with two
pearls and two turquoise stones/beads (Dickson)

خياره **Khiyarah**
تعويذة اسطوانية الشكل Cylindrical amulet box

خلخال **Kholkhal (pl. khalakhil)**
الجمع خلاخيل Anklet

خرز **Khorss (pl. akhrass)**
حبات صغيرة Pendant

خزامه **Khozam (pl. khozamat)**
حلق صغير للأنف Small nose-ring

خرص **Khurs (pl. khirsan)**
حلق للأذن ، الجمع خرصان Ear-ring

خويسات **Khuwaisat**
سوار ذهب سميك Thick gold bracelets studded with turquoise
(Dickson)

كرداله أو كردان **Kirdala (kirdan)**
عقد قصير للرقبة Choker necklace

كتبات **Kitbat**
حبيبات صغيرة من الذهب لتزيين شعر المرأة الثرية Drop-like gold ornaments woven into the hair,
worn by rich women (Dickson)

القرآن الكريم **Koran (Quran)**
كتاب الله الذي أنزل على سيدنا محمد صلى الله علية وسلم ، باللغة العربية Muslim book of the Islamic religion. The word of
God as transmitted by the Angel Gabriel in Arabic
to the Prophet Muhammed

لميا **Lamiya**
حلق طويل للأذن Long pendant ear-ring, eastern and southern
regions (Hawley)

لزم **Lazm**
حلية تلبس تحت الذقن وتمتد من الأذن الى الأذن Ornament worn on chinline from ear to ear and
attached to headgear

لحام **Liham**
لحام شيئ في آخر، عملية اللحام Soldered or soldering technique

لولي **Lulu**
لآليْ Pearl

Ma'ainna
معينة
حلية للياقة تتدلى منها خمس سلاسل
Bead collar with five pendant chains (Dickson)

Ma'azed
مـأزد
سوار لأعلى الذراع من الزجاج الأسود (رواله)
Small black glass armlets, Rwalla (Musil)

Madan mutarraz
معدن مطرز
معدن منقوش
Wrought metal

Mahfur
محفور
وجود حفر على السطح
Engraved or engraving technique

Mahnaka
مهنقة
عقد من المرجان
Coral necklace, Rwalla (Musil)

Mahr
مهر
مبلغ من النقود يدفعه العريس الى أهل العروس
Dowry

Majlis
مجلس
مكان يجلس فيه الناس
Council or audience and by extension, a place where an audience is held

Marami
مرامي
خواتم رفيعة تلبس في مجموعات من إثنين أو ثلاثة أو أربعة
Thin rings worn in groups of two, three and four (Dickson) or silver thumb rings sometimes including small set stone, Oman (Hawley). Syn. with *haismasbukat* and *butham*

Marin
مرن
طري
Plastic

Marjan
مرجان
مرجان
Coral

Ma sha la
ما شاء الله
بناءً على إرادة الله
According to God's will

Maskah
مسكة أو سماكة
تعويذة محفور عليها آية قرآنية
Syn. with *samakah*. Inscribed Koranic amulet

Masri
مصري
مواطن من مصر
Egyptian

Mata'hin
مطاحين
أنواع من الخواتم
Coined and belled ring

Mathayid
مصايد
سوار من الذهب للمعصم أو خلخال للقدم
Plain gold bangles (Dickson)

Mathayid al Haiya
مصايد الحية
سوار ملتوي على شكل الحية
Mathayid with wavy designs (Dickson)

Mazrad
مزارو
عقد بنت عمانية
Omani girl's necklace (Hawley)

Mesbaha
مسبحة
يستخدمها المسلم بعد الصلاة للاستغفار، تحتوي على ٣٣ أو ٩٩ حبة مقسمة الى أقسام من ١١ حبة أو ٣٣ حبة ، يوجد بها عدد إثنين حبة فاصلة كبيرة وفي نهايتها مئذنة .
Syn. with *subha*. Muslim prayer beads sometimes referred to as "worry beads". Strands of 33 or 99 beads in multiples of 11 or 33, divided by 2 space beads and 1 tasselled terminal bead

Milak
ملاك
عقد قران
Engagement contract

Mirjan
مرجان
سوار من المرجان الأحمر
Red coral bracelet (Dickson)

Mizmar
مزمار
Nail or mace-shaped terminal bead Yemen (Kennedy)
خرزه تشبه الصولجان ، في اليمن

Morr
مـر
Myrrh (an aromatic resin from the tree *Balsamodendron myrrha*) was the major ingredient in medicaments and cosmetics in ancient times
مادة صمغية من الأشجار، المادة الرئيسية في الأدوية ومستحضرات التجميل في الماضي

Muakhkhar
مؤخر
Second part of the dowry. A sum promised to the wife in case of divorce
جزء مؤجل من المهر يدفع فقط في حالة طلاق الزوجة

Muqaddam
مقدم
First part of the dowry payment paid at the time of engagement
مبلغ من المال يدفعه العريس الى أهل العروس في وقت عقد القران

Mushabbak
مشبك
Filigree technique
عملية الزخرفة بالتثقيب

Nahas Asfar
نحاس أصفر
Brass
نحاس اصفر اللون

Naqsh
نقش
Chasing technique
عملية تزيين المعدن بالنقوش

Nasf al Qamar
نصف القمر
Half moon
شكل القمر عندما يكون نصف دائرة

Nay
ناي
Flute
آلة نفخ موسيقية

Okd (pl. okud)
عقد
Syn. with *iqd*. See *iqd*
الجمع : عقود ، انظر عقد

Oud
العود
Standard Arabic musical instrument belonging to the family of short lutes similar to a guitar, for sole instrumental music or to accompany a singer
آلة موسيقية عربية من النغمة القصيرة مشابه للجيتار يستعمل بمفرده ، وبمصاحبة المغني

Qat jauharah
قطع الجوهرة
Gemstone cutting
عملية قطع الأحجار الكريمة

Qiladah
قلادة
Pendant necklace
سلسلة تلبس حول الرقبة وبها دلاية

Qimah
قيمة
Value
ثمن

Qirsh
قرش
Copper and nickel coin (the first Saudi coin)
عملة من النحاس أو النيكل، عمله بالمملكه

Qirsh darij
قرش دارج
Copper and nickel Saudi coins (22 equalled 1 riyal)
عملة قديمة بالمملكة من النحاس أو النيكل، كل ٢٢ قرش دارج تساوي ريال واحد

Qsir shift
كسر الشفه
Filigree technique
عملية التخريم والتثقيب

Rabaaba
ربابة
One stringed fiddle
كمنجة لها وتر واحد

Ramadan
رمضان
Ninth month of the *Hejiri* (the Holy month of fasting)
شهر الصوم عند المسلمين، الشهر التاسع في السنة الهجرية

Reysh
ريش
Agate beads from Bombay
حبوب عقيق من بومباي

ريال

Riyal
Saudi silver coin (originally 10 equalled 1 British gold sovereign)

عملة فضية سعودية ، كانت في الأصل كل ١٠ ريال تساوي جنيه ذهب انجليزي

رومي

Rumi
Byzantine

بيزنطي

روماني

Rumani
Roman

رومي ، كاثوليكي

صحاره

Sahhara
Woman's treasure box

صندوق تضع فيه المرأة النقود

صهر

Sahr
Fusing technique

عملية صهر المعادن

سبك

Sakb
Sand casting technique

عملية صب المعادن في قوالب

الصلاة

Salaah
The second of the five tenets of Islam – prayer

ثاني أركان الاسلام الخمسة

صليبي

Salibi
Crusader (adjective)

المشترك في الحملة الصليبية

الصليبيون

Salibiyyun
Crusaders

المشتركون في الحملات الصليبية

سمك

Samak
Fish

حوت

سمكة

Samakah
Syn. with *maskah*. See *maskah*

انظر مسكة

سنكة

Sankh
Necklace of gold coins (Dickson)

عقد من العملة الذهبية

صايغ الذهب

Sayegh al dhahab
Goldsmith

صانع الحلي الذهبية

صايغ الفضة

Sayegh al fiddah
Silversmith

صانع الحلي الفضية

سباط

Sbat
Small black glass bangles, Rwalla (Musil)

سوار صغير من الزجاج الأسود

شف

Shaf
Small nose ornament

حلية صغيرة لتزيين الأنف

شغاب

Shaghab
Hooped ear-ring usually with pendants, northern Oman (Hawley)

حلق للأذن

الشهادة

Shahada
The first of the five tenets of Islam – the profession of Muslim faith:
"There is no god but God (Allah) and Muhammed is His prophet"

شهادة أن لا إله إلا الله وأن محمدا رسول الله

شاهد

Shahid
Forefinger and by extension the ring worn on it or, finger-ring with a point on one side which is worn pointing towards the fingernail and towards Mecca when the wearer utters the *shahada* or, silver ring with large square turquoise (Dickson)

السبابة ، الخاتم الذي يلبس في السبابة

شرقي

Sharqi
Oriental

سكان الشرق

Shawahib شواهب
خاتم يلبس في السبابة ، في عمان
Finger-ring with a point on one side of the bezel, worn on the forefinger in Oman (Hawley)

Shawwal شوال
الشهر العاشر الهجري
Tenth month of the *Hejiri*

Sheikh شيخ
رجل ذو مركز اجتماعي أو ديني
Respected gentleman, tribal leader, religious scholar

Shugl al khurduq شغل الخردق
عمل حبيبات بارزة
Granulation technique

Sidaireeya صديرية
قميص تلبسه النساء في الحجاز، له ياقة مرتفعة وأكمامه ضيقة وتصل الى المرفق .
High collared, elbow-length, narrow-sleeved blouse which serves as a brassiere, vest and cravat. Worn by Hijazi women.

Silk سلك
سلك معدني
Wire

Silsilah سلسلة
حلقات معدنيه متصله ببعضها
Chain

Sini صيني
مواطن من الصين
Chinese

Siwar (pl. asawir) سوار
بناجر لأعلى الذراع
Armlet

Souq سوق
مكان للبيع والشراء
Market-place

Souq al badw سوق البدو
مكان البيع والشراء للبدوي
Bedouin marketplace

Subha سبحة
مرادف مسبحة
Syn. with *mesbaha*. See *mesbaha*

Sundouq hashab صندوق خشب
خزانة خشبية ، تحفظ به المجوهرات ، يسمى احياناً خزانة كويتية أو مدينية
Wooden dowry chest, sometimes called a Kuwaiti or Medina chest

Tahmiyah تحمية
عملية تقوية المعدن بواسطة تسخينه ثم تبريده
Annealing technique

Taler طالر
الطالر: دولار فضي ، عملة ماريا تريزا
Thaler, referring to silver trade dollar, the Maria Theresa coin

Tallal طلال
مشابك شعر
Pendants to *hama* hair ornament (Dickson)

Tamimah deeneyyah تميمة دينية
تعويذة دينية
Religious amulet

Taqleed تقليد
مزيف
False or imitation (as in fake gems)

Tar طار
طبل
Drum

Tarq طرق
عملية طرق المعدن لتحويله الى صفائح مستوية
Hammering technique

Turki تركي
مواطن من تركيا
Turkish

Turzijjl
Copper ear-rings, Rwalla (Musil)

طور زجل
خماخم من النحاس

Tut
Five-sided, clustered "mulberry" style silver beads, Yemen (Kennedy)

توت
خرز فضي يشبه ثمرة التوت

Umla (pl. umlat)
Coin

عملة
نقود

Umm
Mother

أم
والدة

Uwayneh
Blue beads

عونية
خرز أزرق

Wagia
Measurement for metal: 31–32 grammes

أوقيه
للمعدن : ٣١ ــ ٣٢ غراماً

Walad
Boy

ولد
شاب

Wasat
Ring for the third finger (Dickson)

وسط
خاتم للاصبع الثالث

Yusr
Black coral from the Red Sea

يسر
مرجان أسود

Zakhrafa
Embossing technique

زخرفة
عملية وضع النقوش

Zand (pl. zanud)
Armlet

زند
سوار لأعلى الذراع ، الجمع زنود

Zarar
Gold medallion set with turquoise, Muntafiq tribe (Dickson)

زارار
ميدالية ذهبية بها فصوص تركواز

Zarayer dhahab
Set of seven gold buttons threaded on chain where each button position is adjustable as it slides along. Worn cufflink fashion on *sidaireeya*

زراير دهب
زراير من الذهب عددها سبعة توضع على الصديرية

Zarir
Bell. Syn. with *garas*

زارير
جرس

Zelade
Glass "pearl" pendant or necklace Rwalla (Musil)

زلادي
علاقة من الزجاج أو عقد

Zmam
Finger-ring, Rwalla (Musil)

زمام
خاتم للاصبع

Zmejjem
Brass or silver ring worn in the left nostril, Rwalla (Musil)

زميجيم
خاتم من النحاس أو الفضة يوضع في ثقب الأنف

Zorar (pl. zarayer)
Button

زرار
زرار

Zujaj
Glass

زجاج
زجاج

Bedouin Jewellery

Traditional Bedouin jewellery is fashioned mostly from silver and often prominently displays turquoise as an embellishment. Sometimes a red stone is included with the turquoise.

It is interesting that races as widely separated as the Arabians and south-western American Indians and Mexicans have created similar jewellery. So great are these similarities, in fact, that many pieces of American Indian silver and turquoise jewellery could be mistaken for Arabian Bedouin ornaments. The Spanish conquest of Mexico appears to be the vehicle by which Islamic jewellery styles and silver-mounted turquoise were carried to the New World. Arabian designs were quite probably introduced to Spain during the 800 years of Islamic rule and the Conquistadors apparently took its artistic themes with them to the New World. Research has proven that the Spanish brought the art of silversmithing and silver coins to

Mexico. Also, it has been recorded that American Indians did not set turquoise in silver prior to the middle of the nineteenth century, although they did make use of it as a talisman.

Recent American Indian and Mexican silver and turquoise jewellery may be more finely fashioned, but Bedouin jewellery has singular charms; it is bold in design and substantial in size and its distinctively hand-crafted appearance resembles the ornaments of the ancients. This combination of characteristics is most appealing, especially to the Westerner whose revived appreciation for hand-crafted items is strongly evident today. This trend, which has been much analysed and discussed, seems to be an overt expression of dissatisfaction with mass-produced objects that symbolize for some a decadence in modern civilization. It may be that it also satisfies to some extent a growing desire to return to a simpler style of life.

Above: *The* lazm *is a rare piece today – it is a unique ornament designed to be worn on the line of the chin – hanging before the neck like a screen. It is attached to the headgear near the ear lobes. There is nothing quite like it in Western jewellery although trendy Scandinavian ear-rings are now occasionally linked from ear-to-ear by a type of necklace that was fashionable in ancient times. A similar ornament was found in the Jawan excavation in the Eastern Province of Arabia. The stones each side are carnelian, the centre: glass.*

Not only is Bedouin jewellery eye-catching, but it often exhibits praiseworthy skill, too. Arabian Bedouin jewellery is characterized by chains, bells, balls, coins, and strands of irregular-sized, multi-coloured and silver beads. There are colourful stones in simple settings surrounded by fluting or bead work in high relief, snug-fitting bracelets with hinged openings and pinned fastenings, necklaces with plaited hemp ties, and intricate meshed ornaments (often sewn to cloth backings – perhaps to protect the wearer from the sun-heated metal, as much as to preserve the ornament). Other gems and materials used include garnet, carnelian, amber, coral, pearl, agate, glass, faience, gold and brass. Even plastic is used, usually in the form of a bead.

The world knows about the jewellery of the past more from documents than from surviving pieces because changes in fashion, scarcity and the intrinsic value of the metals and gems have caused vast destruction of precious ornaments. Moreover, traditional silver, copper, bronze and brass pieces have fallen victim to corrosion. By contrast, gold's inherent qualities have preserved ornaments where every other trace of a material culture may have vanished. For this reason, gold was long ago given the status of "royal" or "noble".

The history of Arabian jewellery is veiled by tradition – paradoxically, tradition dictates that the jewellery be destroyed on the death of its owner (making it impossible to find very old pieces), yet, this custom of destruction and renewal kept alive a desire for age-old styles and designs.

The Bedouin of the past favoured traditional styles whatever the silver content and workmanship. Pieces often appear in many qualities as a proportion of cheaper jewellery is manufactured to suit the poorer Bedouin's pocket. The item is no less important to the recipient although fine silver has an obvious advantage.

New Bedouin jewellery is sold by the gramme and the price is continually rising. Bedouin women, like all Arab women, are inordinately fond of jewellery and it is rare to see a little girl without at least one bracelet. These days, however, they are more often made of gold. This practical move from silver to gold allows Bedouin women to make a quick transaction in the marketplace. Gold has become easier to sell than silver. In very hard times, even a young girl might be called upon to relinquish her golden trinkets in order to ease her family's financial distress.

It is impossible to fix prices for old Bedouin jewellery because the silver content and workmanship vary so greatly. If a nomadic Bedouin woman in need parts with her jewellery, or her family disposes of it upon her death, she is generally represented in the transaction by a male member of her family. No scales are used in the Riyadh Women's *souq*, so bargaining has a great deal to do with the price he will get. This is also true in Jeddah, where there is no Women's *souq* but the silversmiths do have scales. They buy and sell old silver jewellery by the *wagia*. This weight is said to be between thirty-one and thirty-two grammes and the dealer sells a *wagia* from anywhere between twenty-five and fifty Saudi riyals. What the silversmith-dealer pays the Bedouin is difficult to establish. Silversmiths originally bought worked silver as scrap, and, in fact, continue to melt down whatever Western collectors do not buy.

Foreigners in search of this old jewellery generally make their way to the Women's *souq* in Riyadh, a colourful market run entirely by women. For years this *souq* has been a favourite haunt of expatriates and visitors to the capital. Originally, new and used clothing as well as herbs, spices and an assortment of cooking utensils were sold. Now, the women traders also keep large collections of old silver jewellery and some old gold ornaments. Many of the gold adornments are set with Gulf pearls. Modern gold pieces display cultured pearls from Japan as pearl-fishing in the Arabian Gulf and the Red Sea is rarely practised today – partly because of the ready availability of these Japanese imports. In very recent times Chinese pearls have been added to the merchandise.

Most of the jewellery catalogued here was purchased in Riyadh, where the two large market areas are the Dira and Batha *souqs*. The women's *souq*, in the Dira area, is where the older and more desirable silver jewellery is found; it is surprisingly cheaper than new pieces sold by silversmiths working at the rear of the Batha *souq*. The rising cost of labour and materials is probably responsible for the disparity in price.

The Antiques *souq* in the Dira area, sells wooden Kuwaiti and Medina chests and an occasional pearling chest with its many small compartments. There are wooden camel bowls, too, and copper pots, brass coffee pots, brass and wooden mortars and pestles, coffee-bean roasters, swords, daggers, guns, suits of chain mail and many other interesting ethnic items – sometimes including a piece of Bedouin jewellery.

In these *souqs*, as in market places throughout the Middle East, bargaining is an acceptable and expected procedure. A single bracelet instead of a pair, or an imperfection and a little damage will rarely affect the price. Rather, the rapport that can be built up between buyer and seller, or sometimes the heat and the time of day or year, seems to do so. Shoppers bargain for almost everything in the *souqs* and Westerners enjoy spending hours haggling. Bargaining can add zest to a mundane shopping chore, and, once they become experienced in it, most people enjoy participating in a good-natured exchange over a price. "Getting a bargain" is strangely satisfying. One feels, too, that the Bedouin traders in the Women's *souq* enjoy the exchange with foreign customers just as much as they like concluding a sale. Of course, foreign interest in ethnic items has caused a sharp rise in their prices from which the dealers benefit. It has also resulted in a scarcity of fine old Bedouin jewellery.

Most foreigners in Saudi Arabia acquire a basic Arabic vocabulary, although few achieve fluency. Experience shows that fluent Arabic is not essential for shopping in the *souqs*, but it wise to learn those words that relate to any specific field of interest and to have a good idea of the currency and values (*qimah*) before venturing forth. To be able to count in Arabic is an obvious advantage and courteous greetings and farewells are greatly appreciated by the Bedouin women traders and silversmiths.

In comparison with other *souqs* in Riyadh, the Women's *souq* is a quiet place, perhaps noticeably so because of the bustling activity in the marketplace directly in front. There can be a sense of excitement for foreign visitors in search of jewellery as they pass through the old entrance to the Women's *souq*, despite the fact that they may have visited there many times before. It is a unique sight. There seems to be an air of expectancy among the traders, whose stalls display a fascinating variety: colourful and pungent spices, brilliant-hued dresses (old and new), cooking utensils and ingredients, and Bedouin silver jewellery. Sometimes it is difficult for Westerners to refrain from showing eagerness, but feigning indifference is an important part of the bargaining ritual.

Shelters of wood and corrugated iron offer shade for these Bedouin women, who wear brightly-coloured, full-length, long-sleeved dresses, partly covered by black cloaks. Their greetings are friendly as they invite a customer to sit down with them to examine their wares and do some quiet browsing and haggling. Squatting on an old carpet, screened by rows of hanging silver waistbelts and strands of red coral, blue faience, brown agate, golden amber and silver beads, a customer is dazzled by the choice. All about are dishes laden with a profusion of silver jewellery studded with turquoise and red stones. From the rear of the booth, exotically coloured, embroidered and sequined Bedouin garments spill forth from great treasure chests. The most costly pieces of jewellery are kept in small, closed showcases and little containers. The finest jewellery is brought out only on request or if the dealer considers that she might have a good sale in the offing.

It is fascinating to learn from these women that this jewellery has often come from far away – crafted in the many towns and cities of Arabia. Sometimes it is from other Middle Eastern countries. Stoic nomadic Bedouin women have worn and enjoyed these ornaments while living out their lives in the desert. Now, no less appreciated, albeit by foreigners, the jewellery appears for sale in the capital city of Saudi Arabia.

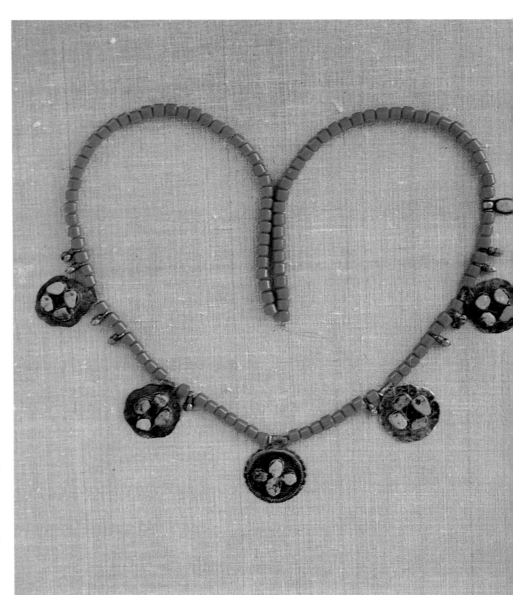

Necklaces

The Bedouin necklace (*iqd* or *okd*), (pl. *iqud* or *okud*) has many forms. Generally they do not have set stones, but rely on beads for colour. Many traditional styles are completely silver. In this case, and sometimes when pearls are predominant, the necklace is finished off with tie cords. It has been hypothesized that many Bedouin necklaces do not entirely encircle the neck, but extend only to where the hair falls in order to save metal and thereby lower the cost. This theory may in some instances have basis in fact but it is not borne out by several traditional styles that are made in all qualities. In the finest versions of *iqd*, where the workmanship is excellent and the silver content is high, the metal ends at the sides of the throat and plaited cotton or a red cloth-bound roll continues

Above: *Brass was often used as a yellow metal substitute for gold. These roughly-made brass medallions are the same size as gold medallions although the precious metal examples traditionally feature only one centrally-set turquoise and not four stones as here. The beads are fake coral. A few tiny brass bell pendants and a turquoise set brass charm also appear on the strand. Most necklaces of this kind have been re-threaded many times and, today, the Bedouin traders commonly thread upon fishing line instead of cotton.*

around the neck to be secured at the back. It seems much more likely that this method of finishing is used because it is more comfortable for the wearer. As for design, it seems aesthetically complete in each case.

A typical Bedouin necklace is generally a large ornament and has many component parts. Pendants are invariable, even on the simplest version which is in fact a pendant (*qiladah*) itself. *Qiladah* are usually set with a stone and this is always red.

The largest necklace of all (*jnad*) is worn in a most unusual way – around the neck and under the left arm. There is no counterpart in Western jewellery. Its pendulous *hirz* and large bells jangle merrily when the wearer moves even slightly. The *jnad* is worn for dancing in the heart of Arabia, whereas a similar ornament in Oman is believed to impart fertility.

The *kirdala* or *kirdan* is a choker necklace or

torque, and this represents a departure from the usual Bedouin necklace in that it is, in one instance, fashioned without pendants. It is claimed as Najdi (Central Arabian), and, in fact, matching bracelets are commonly found there, yet there is nothing quite like it anywhere else on the Arabian Peninsula. An almost identical necklace is seen in Turkey and Afghanistan.

Not a necklace, but covering the neck, is the *lazm*, a unique piece of jewellery worn along the chinline and attached somewhere near the lobes of the ears to the headgear. The *lazm* is constructed from embellished hollow segments which support strands of belled chain. It is a very pretty piece with no counterpart in Western jewellery, although something similar was worn thousands of years ago on the Arabian Peninsula and appears again in modern Scandinavian jewellery. The Peninsula piece was found at Jawan, dated 100AD.

Opposite page: *This style of triangular pendant is worn as a necklace and as a head-dress ornament. The basic triangle changes in the hands of each jeweller. These pieces are from Yemen. The central* stone *may be garnet, carnelian or glass. Tiny hand-shaped charms are known as the hand of Fatimah and these are usually pendant from the triangle. The set red beads are often coral.*

Below: *This pretty necklace from Yemen is freshly strung on cotton. The fake coral beads and silver are quite old and damaged. The trader has been enterprising enough to thread it traditionally* although the central piece *does not appear to belong to the terminal pieces. It is customary for the three main pieces to have identical embellishment. This style is increasingly rare.*

Left: *Similar pendants to these came from various parts of the Peninsula. This particular selection was made in North Yemen. They are old and the applied filigree is very delicate.*

Beads

Beads (*kharaz* – Singular: *kharzah*) have been called eloquent for they act as messengers from remote civilizations. The link between Bedouin traditional jewellery and the ornamentation of ancient civilizations can be shown by means of beads. Mace-shaped beads commonly used in the terminal position in Bedouin jewellery are identical to those used in the same position in Greek necklaces dating from the fourth century BC. The same beads appeared at the Jawan Tomb excavation in the Peninsula, dated about 100 AD and were found in northern Afghanistan in a tomb of approximately the same period. The cowrie shell-shaped bead also found in the Jawan Tomb was peculiar to Egyptian necklaces and girdles of the Middle Kingdom (2040 to 1730 BC), when it was regarded as a fertility symbol and protective amulet for pregnant women. Cowrie shells from the Red Sea or the Arabian Gulf were also common to necklaces worn about 5000 BC.

In the history of man, beads have been important, whether they were made from drilled nuts, seeds, bone, teeth, claws, tusk, shells, fossils, wood or gem material. Beads have been used in tribal diplomacy as peace tokens, for barter and for currency, but primarily they have been worn for decoration.

Early men and women wore beads made of wood, a fashion that is popular again today. Egyptian wall paintings of the Middle Kingdom period depict men drilling stone with bow drills to make beads. With the invention of glazed pottery faience and glass-making skills, the Egyptians were able to imitate a diversity of gem material and became expert at their manufacture, so even the poorest Egyptian of those times owned some kind of bead necklace.

Beads of jade, amber, coral, carnelian, feldspar, lapis lazuli, bronze, glass, ceramic, quartz and faience have been found together with tiny fragments of ancient glass on the surface of archaeological sites in the Eastern Province of Arabia – evidence of the Peninsula's bygone trade in beads from afar. Jade, lapis lazuli, and bronze beads do not now appear in traditional Arabian Bedouin jewellery. Together with costly frankincense and myrrh, beads, real and fake, are known to have been carried along the ancient trade routes. More recently, amber, ebony and bone beads are known to have come from Africa. Bloodstone and carnelian still arrive from Pakistan and glass and wood beads come from India and Pakistan. At Faw in the south-west of Central Arabia, beads from the first–third centuries AD show that rock crystal, limestone, steatite, carnelian, agate, bronze, faience and glass were popular in that period.

Very old and perhaps ancient beads are occasionally found loose in trays of silver jewellery at the Riyadh Women's *souq*. Sifting through the bottom of these dishes has revealed rare "eye" beads, sometimes known as *ain nimr* or "tiger eye". Turquoise is not a common medium for beads in Arabian jewellery. It is usually used in settings. However, pierced, shaped lumps of turquoise do turn up in these trays and these look like ancient Egyptian beads.

Below: *These old beads bear a remarkable resemblance to a style of ancient Egyptian necklace. Most are turquoise beads – some are chrysocolla, a copper silicate, and others are ceramic.*

Bottom: *Amber beads, real and fake, are popularly worn by the Arabian Bedouin. The bead shapes are usually as shown here. The large cubes were once used as currency in neighbouring Africa.*

Colourful beads, strung or pendant, are a common design element of Bedouin (*Badawi*) jewellery, just as they were in ancient Egyptian jewellery. Like the Pharaohs, the Arabian Bedouin wear glass and faience as much as they do garnet, carnelian, coral, amber and agate. Individual value is disregarded. The fact that some red material, whether carnelian, garnet, coral or glass, is used interchangeably by the Bedouin jewellers, stresses the importance of red as a traditional colour, whatever the value may be. Many traditional necklaces (*iqd*) rarely have set stones on silver pendants and rely on beads for their colour.

Characteristic of Bedouin necklaces is the combination of beads of varying colour and size to form the major part of the strand – larger beads and pendants occurring now and again in uniform relief. Graduated strands of beads are unknown and simple, uniform strands are uncommon,

Above: *Most spherical silver beads are fashioned from two embossed halves and most of the embellishment is applied before the pieces are joined. Applied shapes and beaded wire are the most common embellishment. In some cases the bead has been built up from filigree fashioned over a shape – see top pair. Silver beads are customarily placed at intervals on a colourful strand, to appear in relief, often matching mace-shaped terminal beads. Most necklaces have been re-threaded many times and it is rare to find the form of embellishment matching on relief and terminal beads. The other style of bead commonly seen on Bedouin necklaces can be seen on page 47 – a coarse type of granulation is formed into triangles, and this design is usually repeated on the terminal beads.*

except in the case of amber. Multi-stranded coral and sometimes pearls, with relief beads at intervals, are part of the traditional range but it is felt that they are a relatively recent influence from Mughal India or the Ottoman Empire.

The actual source of Bedouin beads is difficult to ascertain. Because of the weight of beads and pendants, necklaces probably break quite often and most have been rethreaded many times; thus, the beads are often mixed – some appear to be very old while others are plastic.

The relief beads in Arabian necklaces are invariably silver (*fiddah*), sometimes as large as 8 centimetres in diameter. These beads are generally formed in two halves by the embossing technique prior to being embellished and soldered together. A few styles of beads are drilled solid silver while some small beads and mace-shaped terminal beads are fashioned from folded metal. Folding is a more economical method of production and such beads are lighter. Other shapes for silver beads include annular, bulbar, cylindrical, spherical, and "seed". Some richly embroidered Bedouin dresses from south-western and western Arabia are embellished with tiny silver "seed" beads. Central Arabian dresses have hollow silver balls decorating sleeve cuffs and smaller silver balls are a feature on one northern Arabian style of Bedouin dress.

Left: *This is not a Bedouin necklace. The beads are, however, from one or more Bedouin necklaces. It is becoming a practice today in Arabia for Western women, and Bedouin traders, to break up traditional necklaces or thread loose beads to make attractive pieces such as this. Even in the south of the Peninsula, where progress has been slower, traders will take apart a traditionally strung necklace to provide sufficient pieces for several pendants. The supporting chains are not silver. The metal is usually called "German silver" which is basically nickel with some copper and zinc added. The beads here are good silver and a substance that has been dyed to resemble red amber.*

Pendants

Pendants (*akhrass* – Singular; *khorss*) are characteristic of Bedouin jewellery and may be coins, medallions, charm cases, balls, bells or elongated beads; in fact, most pendants have further pendants attached. Usually five or seven major pendants form part of a necklace and occasionally the design requires only three. One necklace, worn by Omani girls, generally has nine pendant coins (Maria Theresa *talers*) and one central pendant – sometimes one or two charm cases are added. Since Bedouin jewellery became popular with the Western world, traders are breaking up necklaces in order to supply only one pendant for each necklace.

Multiple pendants are common to the Bedouin jewellery range. This is an ancient fashion and similar pieces were popular with the Egyptian (*Masri*) and Persian (*Ajami*) jewellers in the distant past. Arabian jewellery illustrates an appreciation of ancient style and elegance even today, when the Bedouin are turning to lighter ornaments made of gold, for multiple pendants remain a favoured design element of the new jewellery.

The stones set in pendants for necklaces are red or blue. Gold pendants, worn five or seven to a necklace, are set with turquoise. Brass is also generally set with blue stones. Silver pendants usually feature red stones and occasionally red and blue stones appear together.

Above: *This beautiful silver pendant* hirz *is believed to be from southen Arabia. It bears similarities to work from both Yemen and Oman. The tiny hand-shaped charms suggest Yemen. The red beads are fake coral.*

Left: *The beads in these examples of single pendanted necklace* (qiladah) *are coral, real and fake, agate, real and fake, faience, glass, ceramic, plastic and silver. Both pendant motifs were perhaps created as a result of inspiration received from the moon. On the* right, *an example of an adaptation of the popular crescent shape, and, on the* left, *the phase of the moon so often romanticized by the great poets of Islam – the full moon* (badr), *according to their verses, heralds a night for lovers. The crescent* (hilal) *has become the symbol of Islam and is seen above mosques throughout the world. The half moon* (nasf al qamar) *is an equally popular motif with the Bedouin jeweller.*

Frank Cox

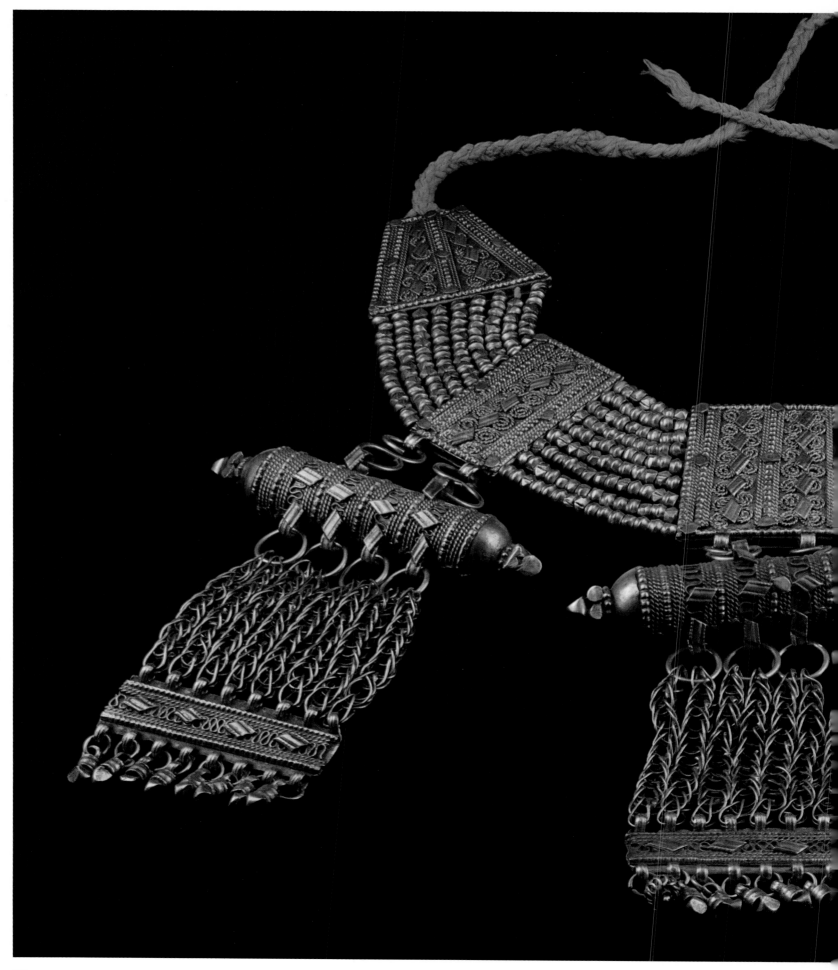

Frank Cox

Left: *This necklace is in original condition and illustrates the Bedouin's ancient method of securing pieces such as this. It has been hypothesized that the silver part on most Bedouin necklaces ends each side of the neck for economy. The quality of silver and amount of work involved in the creation of this necklace belies the theory. It is more likely that this method provides comfort for the wearer. This traditional style invariably supports three hirz or charm cases. Today, they are commonly broken up to provide three separate pendants.*

Charms

As components of jewellery, charms (*ahjibah*, singular *hijab*) have a long history. Charm cases, worn as pendants, were common in Persia in the second and third centuries AD and had both religious and superstitious significance. They enjoyed a period of renewed popularity in Persia in the late twelfth and thirteenth centuries.

Hirz, as they are called in Greater Arabia, are manufactured in a variety of designs and are always used as pendants to a necklace, usually in groups of three or as a central pendant. Some of the finest examples are crafted in the south of the Peninsula. Fashioned without set gems by Bedouin jewellers, *hirz* are not of purely religious import unless there are verses from the Koran sealed inside (the word *hirz*, in fact, originally meant a folded piece of paper with a religious inscription on it). Sometimes, however, the receptacle is quite empty so the ornament is not correctly a Koranic amulet. Yet, a sealed *hirz* of ample size may be set with a large stone that is religiously inscribed; thus it becomes a Koranic amulet (*maskah* or *samakah*) even if the case is empty.

In Palestine, such amulet cases are generally suspended from a silver chain, a custom recently taken up on the Arabian Peninsula. Necklaces originally composed of three *hirz* are now often broken up to supply pendants for three chains. These chains are invariably "cupro" or "German silver", a metal that has no real silver content but is instead an alloy of nickel, tin, zinc and copper.

Talismanic function has always been an important aspect of man's jewellery. Even today, in many parts of the Middle east, small charms are placed on children by their mothers who believe these will give protection from danger and illness. Shelagh Weir, a noted authority on the Bedouin culture has written that green stones (*kharaz al kabseh* or *kharaz al akhdar*) are believed to be an effective way of preventing post-natal infections, whereas white stones (*kharaz al halib*), in the case of a Syrian or Jordanian Bedouin mother, are supposed to promote lactation. Also, in these countries, blue beads (*uwayneh*) and other blue stones are worn as protection against the Evil Eye, upheld in many parts of the world to be the malignant power of the envious. The ancients believed that red stones (*ahjar hamra*) had the power to stop all sorts of bleeding and inflammation. They are still worn in Afghanistan for good health and as protection against eye disease. Red and blue stones probably had significance once on the Peninsula but green and white stones are rare. Green beads and set stones are occasionally found in Hijazi jewellery and are used in Dhofari pieces.

Again suggesting the antiquity of traditional jewellery design in Arabia, is the triangle motif. The triangle was considered the quintessential amulet in the Middle East from earliest times. It is the most common design on Arabian handicrafts. Bedouin who wear traditional jewellery with design elements similar to those of ancient symbolic ornaments, however, attach no importance to them other than as pleasing possessions. Small children find these tinkling ornaments a source of amusement.

Right: *On the Arabian Peninsula, a charm case is called a* hirz, *and this name derives from the fact that an inscribed piece of paper, usually holding Koranic phrases, is known as* hirz. *Charm cases have been popular since ancient times and they are fashioned in many shapes, mostly square, rectangular or cylindrical. Occasionally, a necklace appears supporting a charm case of an unusual shape – in this case the pendant supports two. Perhaps the silversmith based the design for the large charm case on a dagger sheath or the similar powder horn. The heart-shaped charm case is an innovative addition which culminates in a handsome necklace. The style may be much more profound and descend from one that required this combination of shapes for a specific purpose.*

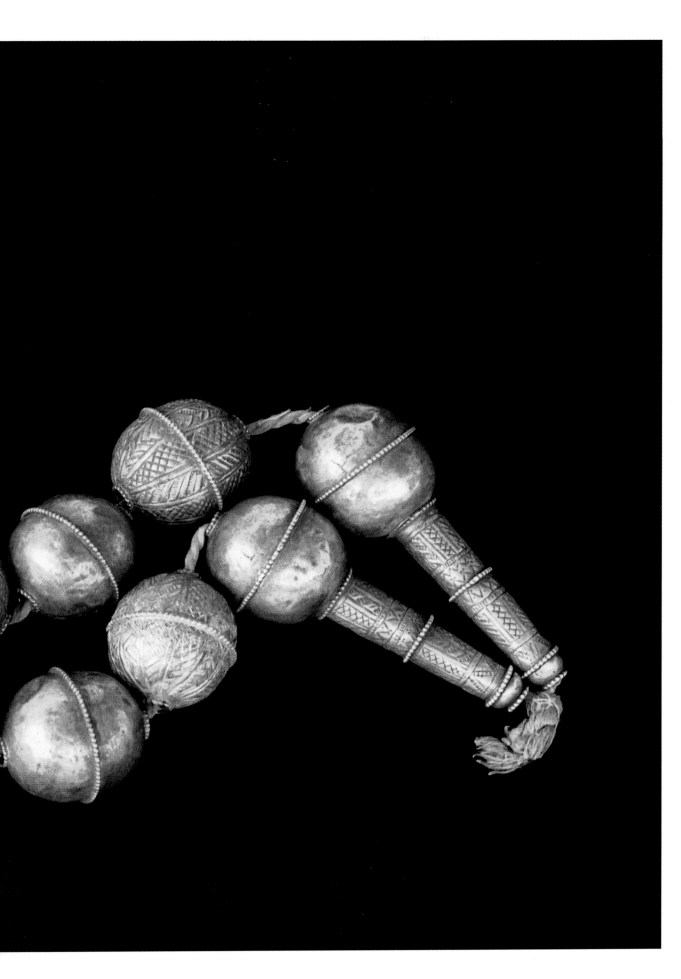

Left: *The largest* qiladah *yet discovered was purchased in the second-hand silver* souq *in Jeddah. It appears to be old but the components are in quite good order. This is due to the thickness of the silver. The central stone on the pendant is red and it appears that four other stones are missing. The surrounding embellishment is applied work – mainly filigree – but the beads exhibit chasing. It is not unusual for beads and pendants on a necklace to have different silver-working techniques so the threading may be original.*
Actual size depicted.

Opposite page: *This massive cylindrical charm case is not sealed. It is created from thick sheet silver overlaid with applied work. The large silver beads are of thinner gauge and of a different quality in both silver and workmanship. It is not unusual to see two different qualities of silver in the chain and other silver on a necklace but it is usual for the beads and* hirz *to be matched on a necklace such as this. It is deduced that this necklace has been put together from odd pieces.*

Right: *An inscribed stone will transform a piece of jewellery into a religious amulet. The central red stone here is engraved with decorative caligraphy containing the word "Allah". Although a large piece, this necklace is delicate-looking; fine filigree and applied tiny shapes decorate the flower-pot shape. The chains are also fine and the supporting section features two set red stones.*

Right: *There is a wide variety of* hirz *on the Arabian Peninsula, and many are made locally. These cylindrically-shaped examples come from Yemen where each silversmith had distinctive styles of embellishment in the past. The oldest pieces display superb craftsmanship. In Yemen, applied techniques were more popular – in Oman, similar pieces would probably exhibit engraving and embossing. Pendant bells are usually missing and each* hirz *is generally sold separately on a base-metal chain.*

Left: *The mobility of Bedouin jewellery as the personal wealth of a Bedouin wife – whether nomad or pilgrim – is confirmed when a necklace such as this is found for sale in Riyadh. It has been established that this necklace was made in Jordan by a well-known Syrian craftsman. The central pendant is a religious amulet by virtue of the inscription "ma sha la" which is translated approximately as "according to God's will". A simple repeated design is gouged out on the reverse side. A religious amulet such as this is known as a* maskah *or* samakah. *Two additional* hirz *are attached at each side and support bells and heart-shaped charms,* hijab. *These cylinders are sealed and there is no way of knowing if they contain religious verses. The supporting chain is unusual and establishes the origin of the necklace.*

Frank Cox

Bells

Bells (*zarir* or *garasat*) – as components of Bedouin jewellery – are attached to bracelets, anklets, belts and rings and are supposed to have originated in Najran in the south of Saudi Arabia. In fact, excavations at Faw, the pre-Islamic city which once served as the capital of the Kingdom of Kindah in south-western Najd, have brought forth an identically-shaped bell (*garaz*) to those attached to present-day Bedouin silver jewellery (the Faw bell is bronze). Artifacts from this site are set at first–third centuries AD and in many cases are clearly of Greek origin. Similar bells were used in an identical fashion by the ancient Greeks in the seventh century BC. They are worn today by the Turkomans of Afghanistan, who believe that their tinkling sound will frighten away harmful spirits. Historically, too, pebbles trapped within the body or the terminals of hollow bracelets, armlets and anklets were believed to repel malevolent spirits by their rattling sound.

Right: *Cumbersome silver "powder-horn" style charm case necklaces are quite rare but there are sufficient of them available to confirm that the design is an established traditional one. The workmanship looks as though it is southern and the finials each end of the horn resemble work from Oman. The pendant cylindrical* hirz *is similar to a Yemeni design but this piece may not be original to the necklace. All of the embellishment is of the applied kind which suggests Yemen. An Omani piece would probably exhibit chasing.*

Coins

While Arabian Bedouin jewellery closely resembles that of long dead civilizations, it adds a decorative dimension of its own in the form of coins (*umlat* – singular *umla*). Silver coins are popularly included, plain or embellished, as finger-ring bezels or as necklace pendants. Five or seven and sometimes nine large coins appear on necklaces at intervals of approximately 8 centimetres.

When coins were first invented, they were worth their weight in whatever metal they were made of; today they are rarely more than tokens. Their function, however, has remained the same.

Taking the place of barter, the earliest coins were crudely fashioned pieces of metal. Before their introduction, the ancient Egyptians and peoples of Mesopotamia were, in fact, using lumps of precious metal; gold, silver, electrum (the natural amalgam of silver and gold) and bronze, which were weighed to estimate the value of commodities. Coins, writes Howard Linecar, evolved in the simplest way from the various pieces of metal used in barter, to blobs of a certain metal of a stipulated weight bearing the sign of a particular merchant. His mark guaranteed that the metal was worth a stated amount. From this method grew the whole system of exchange by money. It is believed that an Ionian merchant first thought of using a sharp tool to impress a lump of gold with a mark that he could recognize when it passed through his hands again. It is recorded that the King of Lydia, who saw the merchants' marks, began to mark his own gold coins with the royal seal (circa 665 BC). The coins of King Croesus of Lydia from the following century are the most famous of the ancient world.

The first Saudi Arabian coin was issued by the Government in 1925. It was a copper and nickel coin called a *qirsh*, minted in the name of Abd al Aziz Ibn Saud as "King of the Hijaz and Sultan of Najd". Other coins in circulation in the area included the British gold sovereign, the gold Trans-Jordanian dinar, the Indian rupee, the Maria Theresa thaler, *taler*, and the Turkish silver majeedi.

In 1928, Saudi Arabia established a bi-metallic independent monetary system of its own, based on the silver riyal and using the British gold sovereign as its standard base (1 sovereign equalled 10 riyals). The riyal was divided into 22 *qirsh darij*. The all-metal currency commanded the confidence of people who traditionally relied on the intrinsic metal content of money.

Full-weight silver riyals were necessary because of fluctuation in the values of the two currencies – and a strong feeling held by the religious authorities that Islamic law forbade coins to circulate at a value above that of their metallic content value. Thus, any significant rise in the world price of silver made it profitable to export the riyal or to melt it down for use as silver bullion. For this reason, in 1935, a new silver riyal of smaller weight and size was struck. At the same time, new silver half-riyal and quarter-riyal coins were issued. None have been minted since 1955 and, as the value of their silver content exceeds their value as coins, they are difficult to find.

The most common *umla* used as a jewellery component is the Maria Theresa *taler* of the Austro-Hungarian Empire (Maria Theresa ruled from 1740–1780). The *taler* weighs twenty-eight grammes and measures forty-two millimetres in diameter. It is the only accepted medium of exchange in many parts of Africa still. Sometimes claimed to be the world's most beautiful coin, it bears the date of the last year of the Empress Maria Theresa's reign, 1780, although it has been struck up to modern times at thirteen mints in Europe and Asia for use as an unofficial trade dollar in areas that lacked a firm coinage – particularly Africa and the Middle East. The word "*taler*" is derived from the Joachimsthaler, a large silver coin of Count Stephen von Schlick in Joachimsthal, Bohemia. The letters "S" and "F", which appear on the standard 1780 *taler*, represent Scholbe and Fabi, the mint-master and warden at Gunzberg, where the taler was minted in the 1760's. With a growing demand for a large silver coin of standard weight and fineness – for commercial and trading purposes – it eventually became a trade dollar. Thereafter it was also minted in Vienna, Prague, Milan, Venice, London, Paris, Brussels, Leningrad, Rome, Bombay and Florence, with an esti-mated one million struck to date. Counterfeits, having a silver content lower than the authentic eighty percent pure, also exist.

The Turkish silver majeedi and Indian coins, once used in the south of the Peninsula, are also incorporated into Arabian Bedouin jewellery. The Indian rupee – a Victorian silver rupee from British India, dated between 1862 and the end of Queen Victoria's reign, 1901, is thirty millimetres in diameter and struck in fine silver. Occasionally the British trade dollar can be found as a jewellery component also. This large silver coin was issued between 1895 and 1935 to promote British commerce in the East. They had been requested for many years by the local bankers and merchants who eventually paid for the costs of production. Approximately the same size as the Maria Theresa *taler* and the British trade dollar, is an Egyptian silver coin minted in the time of Sultan Fuad, the father of King Farouk, this is seen occasionally as a jewellery pendant. Each of these coins are invariably badly worn because fine silver is soft. They are barely recognizable because of this or as a result of detail being obliterated by embellishment. It is interesting to discover which coins circulated in the Middle East early this century.

Right: *Coins, umlat, are used as pendants on Bedouin necklaces – usually five to a strand. The most popular coin (umla) is the Maria Theresa* taler *which is often so heavily encrusted with decoration that it can barely be recognized. Glazed blue ceramic beads interspersed with pendant silver balls divide these coins. The mace-shaped terminal beads are traditionally placed.*
Below: *A traditional Najdi necklace is made up of a double strand beginning each side of the neck. It is closed with a cotton loop over an agate bead. The central pendant is gold set with turquoise and the other pendants are pressed gold "sequins". The beads are coral, turquoise, agate, silver, gold and faience. Pendants of agate occur here and there with silver* hijab.

Bracelets, Armlets, Anklets and Belts

Bracelets, armlets and anklets are always worn in pairs. Pairs of bracelets (*banager* – singular *bangar*) and armlets (known as *asawir* – singular *siwar*) and anklets (*khalakhil* – singular *kholkhal*) can be found to match in style even now. The armlets are somewhat larger than the bracelets and the anklets are larger still.

One particular design, common in the Eastern Province, is a hoop which features thimble-shaped projections attached to the body of a cast anklet. These are covered almost completely with clustered nodules which could have been cast at the same same as the bracelet or the decoration could have been formed later by fusing on beaded wire or small spheres. Certain bracelets of a traditional style are created by different methods and it seems to depend on how the individual silversmith believes he can best achieve a design. Although these cast anklets are very heavy, weighing ap-

proximately 200 grammes, they are quite delicate-looking in comparison with the more common woven variety favoured in the south-west of the Arabian peninsula. In this style, the anklet and bracelet have a hinged and pin-fastening closure, which is also seen in Oman. In some styles, it is only the anklet that requires such an opening. The bracelets slip easily over the wrist in most cases, while a matching necklace is usually completed with a cotton cord tie or chain. One or two Central Arabian bracelets are purposely snug-fitting and have hinged and pinned closures.

According to Ruth Hawley, there is an enormous variety of styles worn in Oman and the most common design is the one with a continuous line of projections divided by a vertical line of four dots. Sur, particularly, specializes in bracelets and anklets featuring projections. *Banagiri* is the Omani word for bangles and *hajala* is also used.

Bedouin bracelets and anklets are correctly worn in pairs. Often the ornaments for wrist and ankle are made in matched sets and only the size will indicate where a piece should be worn. As a general rule, anklets have hinged and pinned fastenings while bracelets slip over the hand. This is not always the case, however. The pair of fine silver bracelets shown here illustrate the geometrically-shaped terminals that may have evolved from bulbous stylized animal heads once popular on jewellery – a style that descends from the Scythians of Central Asia.

70

Left: *Saudi Arabian silver riyals are commonly soldered to Bedouin jewellery and such coins are often the focal point of the design – as they are on these bracelets. The external surfaces of these light-weight* asawir *are crudely chased with a geometric design, and the terminals, partially hidden by the coins, are domes fashioned by hammering a disc of silver in a concave mould – the technique of embossing.*

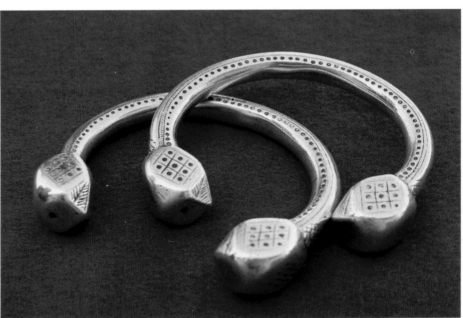

Left: *Solid silver horseshoe-shaped armlets are terminated with heavy geometrically-shaped finials. The design is similar to that seen on the hollow bracelets on page 68. Simple scoring with a graver, and a repeated design chased with a decorative punch have embellished this elegant style.*

Silversmiths also make waist belts (*ahzimah*) that are woven and belled to match some styles. Such a waistbelt weighs approximately two kilograms, and is kept for special evenings when there is a celebration. It is a particularly Oriental characteristic to add bells or include tiny objects in hollow jewellery, and these add greatly to the enjoyment of the swaying Bedouin dance. In Oman, it is said that these are to warn a man that women are approaching. Yet another style which forms a complete set is similar to Celtic jewellery; it is a twisted wrought design and the necklace is a torque-like choker. The matching waistbelt (*hizam*) is very rare today and its design is unique amongst the broad range of Bedouin silver belts. Carnelians are set in a central "buckle" and a belled fringe of chain hangs from the centre of the back. This unyielding style of belt is difficult to put on. The opening is narrow in similar fashion to a torque.

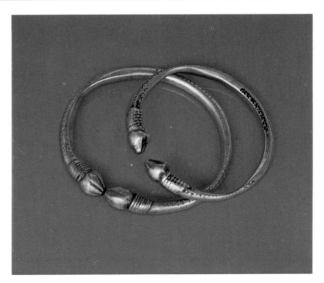

Left: *Armlets and anklets of this thin wrought style are invariably large in circumference. Several pairs are often worn at the same time. Matched pairs are hard to find but this is not important because the chased geometric designs are very similar as a rule, and usually lightly done. On these examples, the designs are quite deep. The terminals resemble snake heads. In this style, the metal is usually good silver.*

71

Below: *Delicate and skilful chasing creates geometric designs and floral motifs. The* *original shallow incised designs have worn because of the softness of good silver.*

Below: *A smooth and silky patina has come with use to these crusty silver bangles.*

Lavish applications of granulation and filigree make up this ornate old pair.

Right: *This pair of light-weight bracelets,* asawir, *have been hammered to roundness over a core of pitch. When this work is complete, the pitch is removed by heating. Identical decorative shields appear on both sides of each bracelet and these caps extend on one side to hide a pin clasp. Orignally, the pins were attached to "safety" chains which are now missing. Silver granules form triangles at each side of a turquoise set in high relief on each shield. Pebbles have been trapped inside the bracelets. It was once a custom to include rattling objects in the belief that sound would ward off evil spirits.*

Frank Cox

Right: *Solid thimble-shaped projections clustered with nodules have made these wrought horseshoe bracelets extremely heavy. Projections as a design element are claimed as south-eastern yet bracelets from this region are normally hollow. This style has been for sale for years in the Najd which may offer a clue to their origin.*

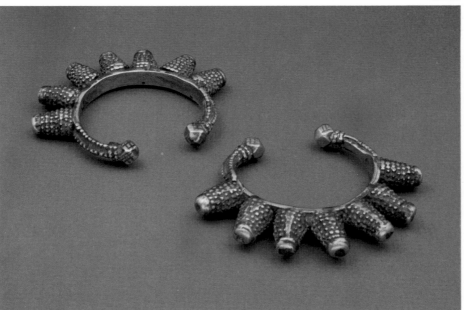

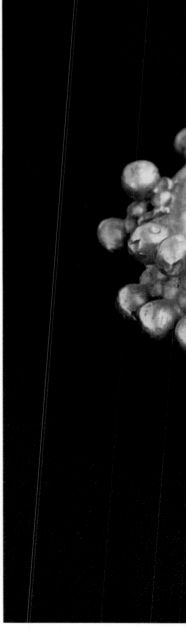

Frank Cox

Right: *Arabian bracelets sometimes suggest a strong influence of another culture. This ornate pair are Central Arabian but resemble work from the Far East. The same style is accomplished by different methods – in this case the domes are hollow – having been formed from filigree. Tiny blue beads are set in an unusual floral motif on the clasp. Quite often this style is quickly and cheaply made from low-grade silver – the domes are merely embossed and decorated with applied work.*

Left: *Solid hoops are heavy but sometimes the decoration can make such bracelets into very pretty pieces. The central red stone is perhaps glass as the red beads on each side are ceramic. The finest silver examples may have garnet or carnelian as a central stone and coral beads would adorn each side.*

Right: *Leather and silver ornaments are popular in the south-west of the Arabian Peninsula. Head circlets and bracelets are embellished with silver medallions and buttons as well as red stones. They are worn by both sexes.*

Above: *Bold styling makes these armlets distinctive. The tribe to which they belonged originally may have been recognized by wearing them. In the past, men on the Arabian Peninsula wore as much jewellery as women. In some remote regions, men still wear ornaments which are traditional for their tribe.*

Left: *Waistbelt styles are
many and varied but they do
fall into a few well-defined
categories. Generally, all
silver waistbelts from the
Peninsula are fashioned from
segments. These pieces are
either threaded over webbing
or they are linked together.
Examples from surrounding
countries are found today
amongst Arabian styles and it
is difficult sometimes to
ascertain which are locally-
made. Most have set red
stones and coins applied to
the body of the belt. Further
confusion occurs when the
coins are foreign. It appears
that Arabian Bedouin women
did wear silver belts imported
from India and Turkey – both
considered traditional. The
belt shown here is by no
means the most beautiful but
it is very interesting. Plaited
silver "webbing" is typical of
Turkish belts; the applied
filigree "flowers" are seen on
bracelets believed to have
originated in Ethiopia; and
the set carnelians look
distinctly Yemeni.*

Head-dress Ornaments

Throughout centuries, women have worn a fascinating array of ornaments in their hair but none have been more original than the Bedouin jewellery pendant known as an *ilagah*. Bedouin women wear them for decoration and to hold their headdresses in place. They are made in many designs using lengths of chain, bells and gemstones. Stones, when they are incorporated into an *ilagah* design, are red or blue and blue predominates. Correctly, they are worn three at a time, one on the back of the head and one at each side, attached by hooks to a circlet (*isaaba*). Sometimes only the two side pendants are worn. Circlet headbands, or diadems, were once popularly worn by Bedouin women and some have five fixed pendants attached – three long and two short – and each is multi-stranded. Plain circlets, *asayib*, are sometimes fine silver or leather decorated with silver.

also handsome; the prettiest seen today, is undoubtedly the Central Arabian *hilyat shaar* – a series of chains that drape at the back of the head. The lowest chain supports a row of bells which continue around two sides of each of two rectangular decorated plates that terminate the chains. Hooks behind these plates affix the *hilyat shaar* to the headgear. *Hilyat shaar* can also be tiny jewels. Although such ornaments were once commonly fashioned in silver, they are rarely found today in anything but brass, but the set stones are invariably turquoise. It was customary to wear them seven at a time at the back of the head. Tresses were threaded through loops at the top and bottom.

The most intriguing head ornament is a kind of hat pin, the spike of which is a porcupine quill. The decorative capping is silver and supports

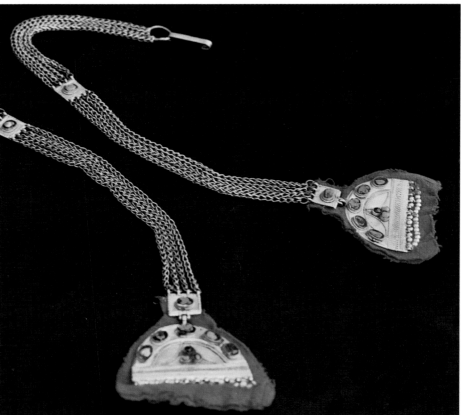

Far left: This oval, slightly convex, 24 kt. gold kaffat, or khamasiyat for the forehead is worn stitched to a protruding unhemmed red cotton backing – probably to keep the metal off the skin as much as to prevent the pearl pendants catching in the hair. The pendants are Gulf pearls pierced with gold and occasionally this traditional piece includes tiny beads in this fringe. The set stones on the body of the ornament are invariably turquoise and quite often two red stones are included.

Left: These two head-dress pendants from Central Arabia were once part of a more elaborate head ornament including a kaffat. The two pieces are worn hanging one over each ear as ilagahs. These examples are mounted on red cotton and display turquoise, red stones and pearls. While the pendants are gold, the chains are silver – no doubt because low-grade silver is strong.

Rich desert women traditionally wore very elaborate gold head ornaments (*hamat* – singular: *hama*), which are still sold in the Riyadh Women's *souq*. These are often fine gold, encrusted with semi-precious stones and fringed with pearls. The various sections of the complete jewelled headdress are connected by chains. Lady Anne Blunt described a nineteenth-century Hayil lady as wearing, not only a mass of gold chains studded with turquoise and pearls around her neck, but also a small gold plate-like forehead ornament about four inches in diameter. This was studded with turquoise. Lady Anne described it as fastened back with gold and pearl chains to another ornament resembling a lappet (also of gold and turquoise), which was hooked on behind the head to flaps that fell each side of the face and ended in long strands of tassled pearls.

Poorer women wore silver headgear which was

bunches of silver balls. A similar silver pin has a twin and these are joined together by chains and each is connected to an *ilagah*.

Both Dickson and Hawley describe head ornaments of great beauty and in both instances, the pieces are threaded into the tresses. Colonel Dickson writes of gold head pieces that are traditional to the Eastern Province of Arabia and Kuwait. Such jewellery is still popular in Bahrain and other places in the Gulf. Ruth Hawley tells of Omani hair ornaments that are supported in the plaits by a pad of goat hair. These Omani pieces are of a totally different design to any other worn on the Arabian Peninsula. Throughout the Peninsula, although the styles for hair ornaments vary greatly, they share the fact that they are all jewellery designed to be worn as adornment on the head – a characteristic that is rare amongst jewellery in the world today.

Below: *An* ilagah *is usually hooked into the head-dress and hangs to sway with movement. The most elaborate are worn on festive occasions when there is dancing. This example is unusual in that it includes a chained section which is worn as a head circlet to keep headgear in place. The bell pendants, fringed with chains and balls, are a higher grade of silver than the chains. Hand-made chain (silsilah) is a principal element of Bedouin jewellery and it often forms the major part of a piece.*

Right: *Correctly, three matching* ilagahs *are worn by Bedouin women. One hangs each side of the head and one hangs down the back. They are commonly hooked to the headgear. Occasionally, old examples are found and the three pendants are joined and attached to a headband. This headband is said to be worn around the face, and the end pendants are missing – they would be attached to each end near the ears. The set carnelian would be worn centre-crown. It may be a tie-cord that is missing making this band a circlet.*

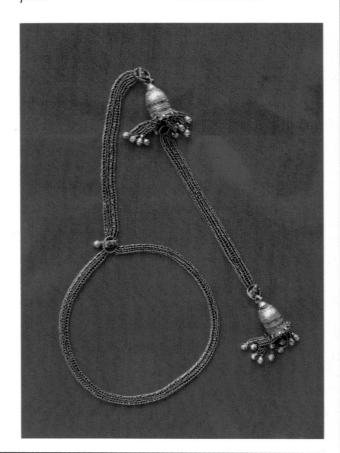

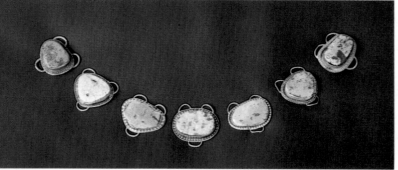

Above: *Pieces such as these* hilyat shaar *are usually found in brass as they are no longer popular and the silver examples have been destroyed. The central five are* silver – the others brass. They *are invariably set with turquoise but the gold pin, centre, is rare. Tresses at the back of the head are threaded with seven pieces.*

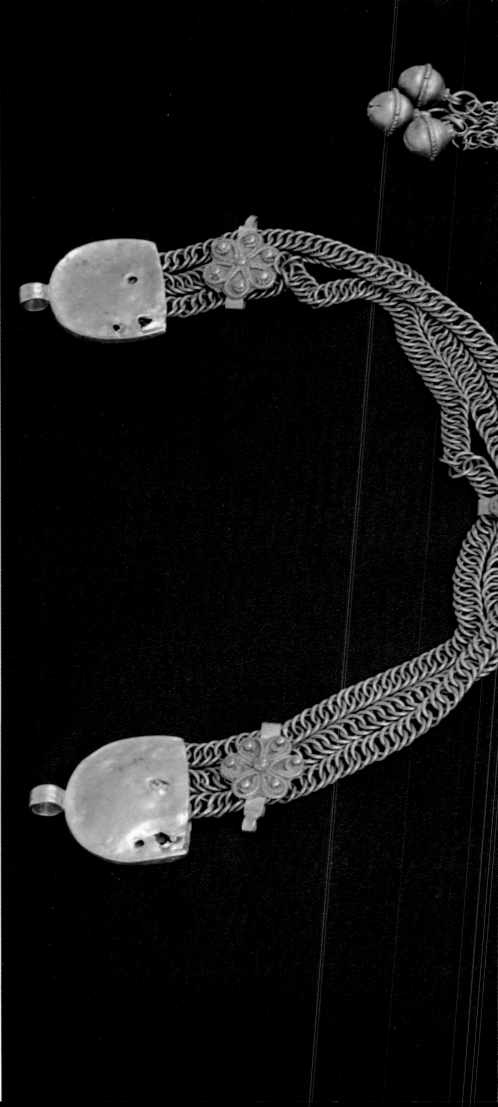

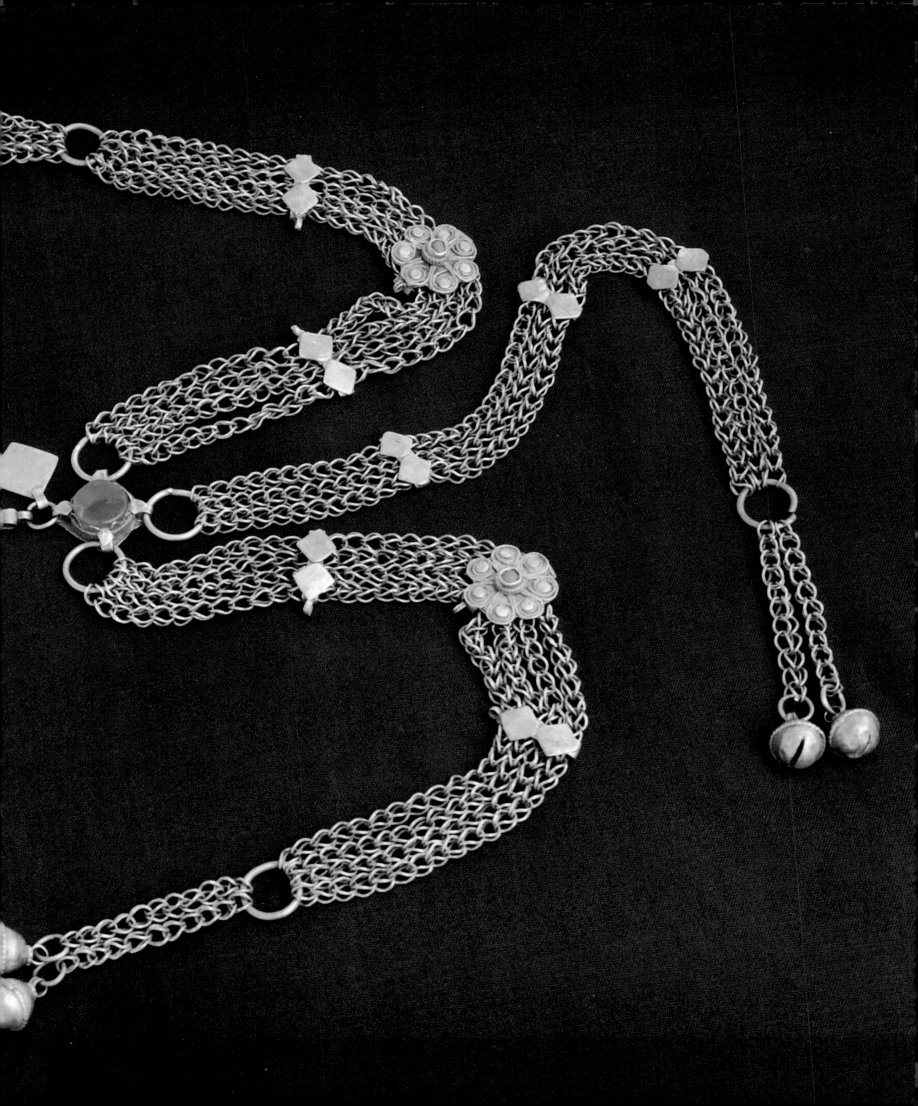

Left: *Yemeni women's head ornaments are usually silver and often quite novel as well as beautiful. These pieces are worn as "hatpins" and known as* mashaaga. *They are, however, stuck into headgear, not hats. One end is silver, decorated with bands of twisted wire, fused around the pin and dividing clusters of silver balls fixed with rings. The other end is usually a porcupine quill. These examples are broken or missing and one has been substituted with a rolled piece of metal. The quills in the picture are from an Arabian peninsula porcupine at the Khamis Mushayt Zoo. Although these* mashaaga *are said to be Yemeni, they were found in Riyadh amongst old Najrani Bedouin jewellery. They are now rare ornaments and may have been popular in many parts of the Peninsula in the past.*

Right: Although Western women like to wear this style of ornament on the bodice of a dress, the plates attached at each shoulder, and some Bedouin women think this is a good idea, die-hards insist that it should be worn at the back of the head — the hooks behind each side-plate to be firmly affixed just above the temples. It is another style of hilyat shaar *or hair ornament and claimed as Central Arabian. Examples have been found, however, in Jeddah's second-hand silver souq. It is most definitely a product of Arabian Peninsula silversmiths. This style of chain with silver balls is a feature of Bedouin jewellery from outside the Peninsula, but the types of embellishment on the plates — applied filigree and shapes — are typically Arabian.*

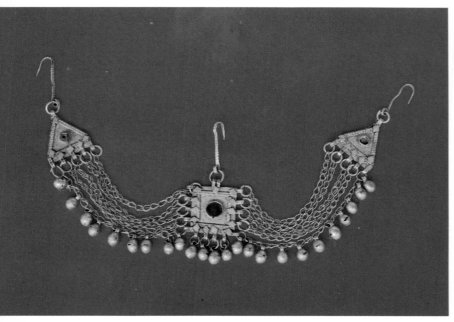

Above: The kaffat, *or forehead ornament, is a very flattering ornament but it is rarely worn today. This is a sad passing. Most traditional Bedouin pieces have modern counterparts — it is the hair and head ornaments that have faded into history. This chain and belled example is delicate-looking and one of the prettiest examples. Unfortunately it is poor silver. The red stones are glass. The central hook is affixed to the headgear at centre-front and the side hooks are attached over the ears, draping the chains just above the eyebrows.*

Above and right: Bedouin jewellery designed to adorn the forehead is often made of white metal without set stones. Well-set stones are usually red, and open collets can house red or blue beads — these are often missing because there are no claws or the collet edge is not turned over. The kaffat, *right, is flexible because it is formed from meshed metal segments to which diamond-shaped pieces have been affixed. These pieces and the terminal sections are embellished with an applied silver-working technique requiring metal to be fused.*

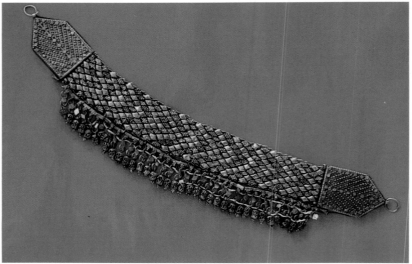

Frank Cox

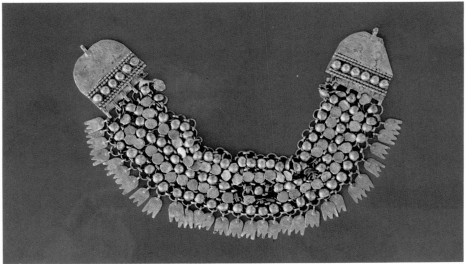

Left: *In line with the Arabian custom of providing traditional jewellery styles in all qualities to suit the means of each family, a silversmith has apparently put this* kaffat *together quickly. The silver content is accordingly quite low. Simple embossing, attractively placed, has been employed to decorate the terminal sections – and the right-hand piece appears to have been cut from a short end. The meshed links common to this flexible style are overlaid with discs and domes. Hand of Fatimah charms are pendant.*

Above: *The pendant on an* ilagah *is designed to weight this chained ornament in order for it to sway nicely when suspended from the headgear. Traditional styles include the bell shape but this is not common. Coins are also uncommon. The amber bead example is quite rare yet effective. A low-grade silver coin completes the pendant – it is obsolete currency, dated 1357 Hejiri 1938 Gregorian. The triangle is by far the most popular shape for pendants – in antiquity it was considered amuletic. The central bar design is seen occasionally.*

Below: *Unique head-dress ornaments from Yemen. The connecting chain is worn* *behind the head and the pendants fall each side of the face as* ilagahs.

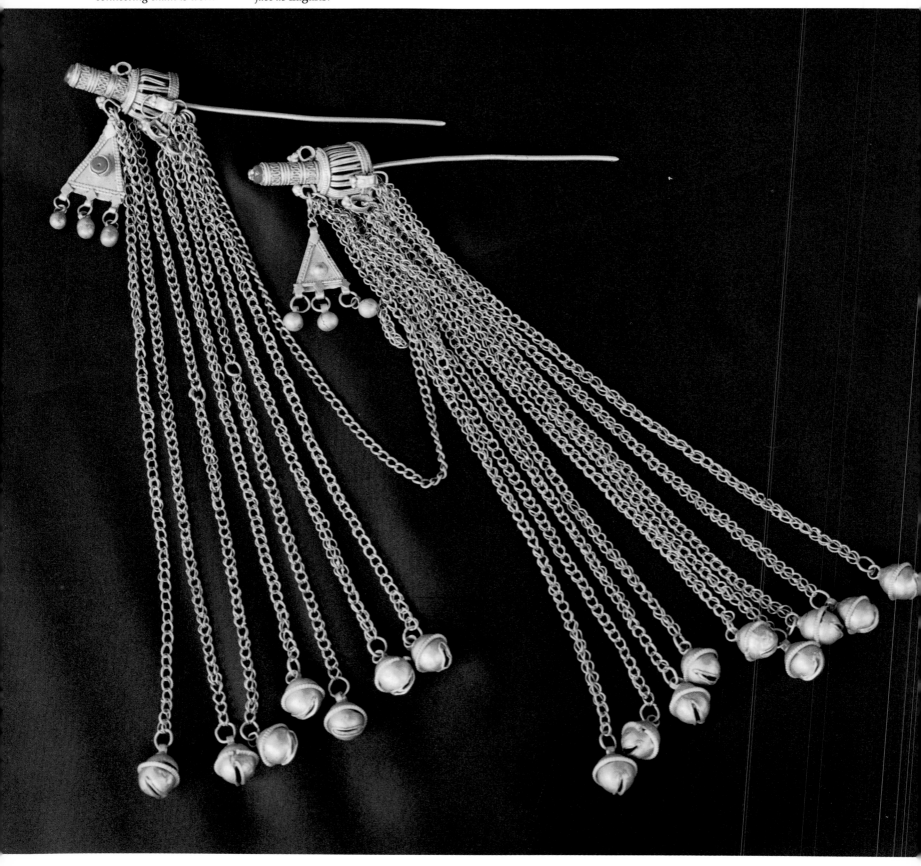

Nose and Ear Ornaments

Left: *This ear-ring style is known as* halaq *or* khurs. *Its pair is unfortunately missing. The silver is particularly fine and the workmanship good. The decorative girdle is applied work – engraving and chasing are rarely used to embellish ear-rings. Filigree and granulation are more usual.*

Below: *Embossing is a silver-working technique used to raise domes for ear-rings. The bottom section of these bells is formed from filigree that supports a band from which fringes of chains and bells are pendant.*

Left: *Ear-rings of this style are usually worn through the ear lobes – some styles are attached to headgear.*

Above: *This Najdi style ear-ring is made in silver or gold – turquoise and pearls decorate gold examples.*

To further adorn themselves, Bedouin women often have one nostril pierced, but this practice is not quite so commonplace as the custom of piercing the earlobes. Bedouin women today favour tiny gold flower-shaped studs for nose ornamentation and these are usually decorated with turquoise and pearls; sometimes red stones are incorporated. These nose-rings and similar earrings come from the Indian subcontinent and seem to be preferred at the moment to the cumbersome traditional styles. A small nose ornament is called *shaf* or *khazama* and a large nose jewel is known as *fraida*.

In the remote regions of Saudi Arabia, the traditional nose ornaments are either a large silver hoop or a semi-circular wire shank attached to a half-moon (*nasf al qamar*). These are worn on one side of the nose – whether on the right or left side depends on the tribe. Far to the south-east of the Peninsula, women seem to favour hoops, whereas the half-moon shapes, so popular with the women of Libya and other North African countries, are worn universally. Both styles were common in Byzantine times and probably passed into the Islamic world with the spread of the Ottoman Empire.

An observer of the early Arabian scene, Lady Blunt, who visited the Peninsula with her husband in the late 1870s, described one particular type of nose-ring they saw in Hayil: "It was larger than those worn in Baghdad or elsewhere, measuring one half to two inches across, worn in the left nostril, consisting of a thin circle of gold with a knot of gold and turquoise attached by a chain to the cap or lappet, also of gold and turquoise". She noted that the ornament was taken out and left dangling when the wearer wished to eat or drink. It appeared to her that the larger the diameter of the nose-ring, the higher the rank of its wearer – as she saw only smaller rings worn by inferiors. It could, of course, have been simply a matter of wealth.

In Oman, young girls sometimes wear ear-rings suspended on chains hanging from their heads. Hooped-shaped ornaments identical to the traditional Bedouin nose decorations, but worn in the ears, are called *halaq* or *khurs* (pl. *khirsan*). In Southern Arabia, a woman's ears may be pierced three times (once near the top of the ear and in two more places further down the lobe) in order to display three sets of ear-rings at one time, currently a fad with both men and women in parts of the Western world.

Southern ear-rings are often novel, no doubt due to multiple influences. The hooped *halaq* is worn and bedouin call it *shaghab*. In northern areas of Oman versions are usually trimmed with pendants. The east coast has produced the *lamiya*, a long chained style, totally different to any other Arabian ear-ring.

Traditional silver ear-rings and nose-rings lost popularity sometime ago and are rarely seen today anywhere near the modern cities. In fact, the old custom of piercing the nose has all but faded away amongst the townspeople of the Kingdom of Saudi Arabia.

Frank Cox

Below: *Hoop ear-rings are perhaps the most common style of traditional Arabian* *ear-ring. They were worn by both men and women. A cone terminal bead is the usual* *closure – the shaft closes into this. The coiled wire decoration is popular.*

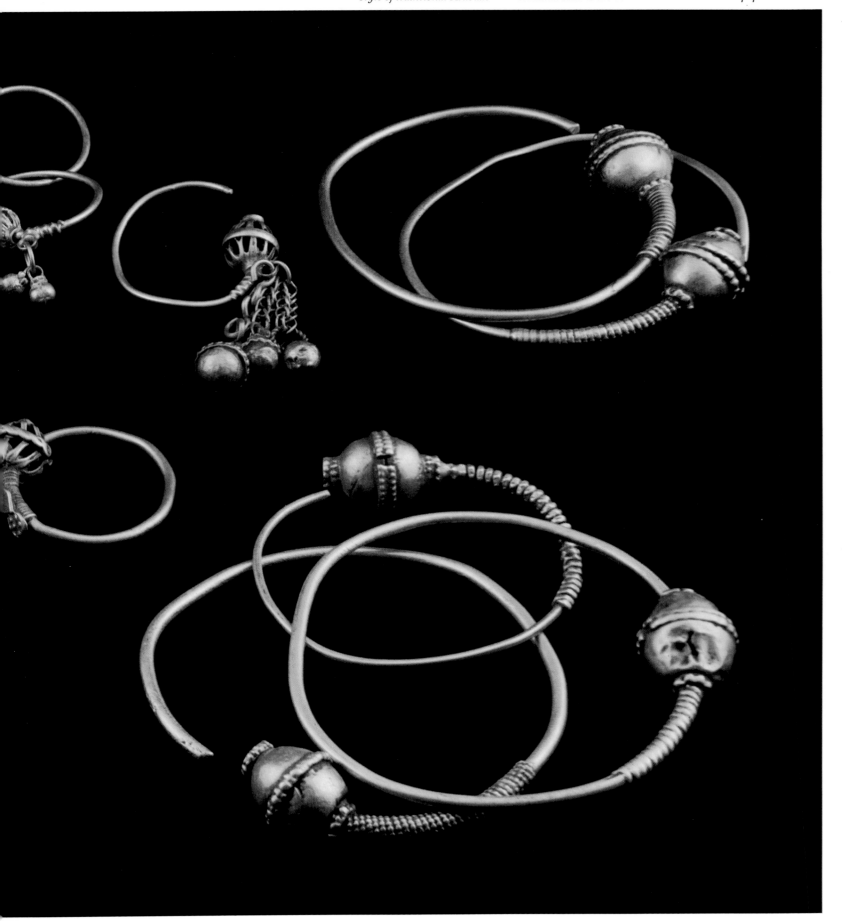

Left: *Silver chains and balls with crusty applied work on the body of these ear-rings make sophisticated pieces of jewellery worthy of the most discerning. Tiny charms are also pendant along the lengths of chain and these are formed from filigree. The design relies on the clustered effect created by these chains which sprout from the centre of the body of the ear-rings to cascade over the chain fringe. It is likely that a Bedouin woman would also wear these pieces fixed into her headgear as ilagahs. While many women in the past had their ears pierced in several places along the lobes to display more than one pair of ear-rings, it was also the custom to attach some styles to head-dress ornaments or to the actual head-dress. Bedouin women today usually have their ears pierced in one place only and wear small gold studs – others still exhibit distended holes in their ears as a result of wearing heavy traditional styles. These particular ear-rings are believed to have been made in the southern part of the Peninsula.*

Finger-rings and Toe-rings

Bedouin finger-ring styles are many and varied: characteristic are large stones, high bezels and richly decorated shanks and shoulders. They often incorporate pendant bells and the result is bold and colourful jewellery.

Finger-ring craftsmanship often brings all the jewellery-making techniques into play as each section of a ring is generally decorated. The hoop of a finger-ring is known as the shank and the upper part is the bezel. The encompassing band, which usually holds a stone, often filed away to make claws, is the collet and the pieces that are attached sometimes to both shank and bezel are called shoulders. The shank is sometimes cast but is usually wrought. The bezel is invariably decorated and sometimes incorporates a stone, either held by claws or glued inside an encompassing band that has been cut from hammered and annealed metal. The shank and shoulders on Arabian Bedouin finger-rings generally exhibit heavily encrusted relief decoration achieved by several techniques.

Classifying Bedouin finger-rings (khawatim – singular: khatim) is a problem similar to that faced by experts when they endeavour to classify ancient finger-rings. The puzzle occurs because a finger-ring often serves more than one purpose and the difficulties are compounded by a lack of documentation. Although the Bedouin sometimes still wear old rings, they cannot clearly remember too much about them. In the not too distant past, finger-rings, although considered to have been mainly decorative, often had amuletic value as well. Moreover, they were often worn, by tradition, on certain fingers for a specific function or symbolic reason. Even today, in the West, although there is a special finger for the wearing of the wedding ring, no one is certain where this practice originated and why.

H.R.P. Dickson, a noted Arabist, writes that up to four rings are worn on one hand at one time. There is evidence which indicates that there was once a strict order for finger-ring placement. In Arabia, today, as many as can be managed are worn by Bedouin ladies for festive occasions. According to Dickson, the names, number and placement of rings vary greatly throughout the Middle East. He gives the following names and placements for Bedouin finger-rings in Kuwait and Eastern Arabia: khamzar is a ring for the little finger, wasat refers to a ring for the third finger (silver or gold and set with a large square or oval turquoise), marami are thin rings (plain silver or gold), worn in threes for the second finger and the al shahid (a silver ring with a large square turquoise) worn only by well-to-do Bedouin ladies.

Shahid is actually the term for the forefinger in Arabic, so called because some Muslims point this finger when uttering the Shahadah, the Islamic doctrinal formula. One silver ring with a point on one side of the shank is also referred to as al shahid. This point is worn facing the finger nail. It is likely that this name applies to other types of rings if they are worn on the forefinger. There is one other Arabian silver finger-ring clearly connected with

Frank Cox

Left: *The six finger-rings in this picture are perhaps the most interesting among Arabian Bedouin traditional styles. Bottom Right, the al shahid displays bells and a centrally set red stone. Left, a rare green stone ring and a fine old example of a high-bezelled set stone ring. The strongly-made silver coin rings are the newest addition to the traditional range – when coins became available, they were mounted belled or plain as were these Saudi coins and Indian rupee respectively.*

Generally stones in Bedouin finger-rings are used in flat form and rarely is a cabochon incorporated. At the Faw excavations in south-western Najd, first – third century cabochon cut and polished carnelians were found. While some of these are thought to be insets for eye-sockets of statues, others were probably meant for finger-rings.

The most common semi-precious stone set in Bedouin finger-rings is turquoise. Carnelian, often known as cornelian (*aqiq ahmar*), an orange to brownish-red colour, is also seen in Arabian rings. Adherence to tradition has played an important role in preserving the use of red and blue stones for the embellishment of Bedouin jewellery, just as it has been responsible for the continuation of jewellery styles.

Bedouin women do not traditionally receive rings as a symbol of betrothal, although the majority of a Bedouin women's jewellery – which includes finger-rings – comes to her effectively as a wedding gift. However, as far back as the Prophet's time, finger-rings were associated with weddings and *mahr* (dowry) and there is an Islamic injunction that requires Muslims to offer rings to their brides as a minimum presentation. Traditionally, Bedouin women of central Arabia receive bracelets as marriage tokens rather than rings.

Betrothal rings first appeared in Roman times and have continued down through the ages as a symbol of marriage – although the forms of marriage rings have changed often. The plain bands of today are a relatively new innovation and the custom of exchanging them is very recent indeed. The exchange of rings between husband and wife, or at least the supplying of a wedding band to the bride, is now customary in Saudi Arabia.

In Oman, writes Ruth Hawley, sets of ten special rings may be presented to a bride. These include five styles which are traditionally made in pairs – in order that the same design appears on the same finger and thumb of both hands. The first finger is reserved for the *shawahib* – the ring bezel is round on one side and pointed on the other – obviously the counterpart of the *shahid*. A convex bezelled silver ring, *khatim abu fauz*, is worn on the second finger; the *khatim abu saith mrabba* is a square-bezelled ring for the third finger; the *haisa*, a coloured stone or silver mulberry-style pyramid ring is worn on the fourth finger; and a silver band, sometimes set with a small stone, is worn on the thumb. Such a ring is known as *marami, hais masbukat* or *butham*.

Toe-rings (*khawatim* – as finger-rings) do not appear to have been worn in all parts of the Arabian Peninsula; they are not mentioned by the early explorers, although there are accounts of their appearance in southern regions. Toe-rings would seem to be an African influence rather than truly Arabian because they are worn in neighbouring Africa but it is not a custom in Central Arabia. A toe-ring is generally recognized by its large size and squared outer shank. They are usually decorated but without a bezel. In Dhofar, the straight side of a "D" shaped toe-ring is worn upwards and a simple ring may be worn beside it to the outside to act as a keeper.

Islam and this can be worn rightfully only by men who have completed the *Haj*. These rings are now rare.

The Bedouin women of central Arabia call all real and fake turquoise rings *fawariz* – a name obviously derived from *fairuz*, the Arabic word for turquoise. One attractive piece of Bedouin jewellery consists of five rings, one for each finger and one for the thumb – all connected by links to a decorative patch on the back of the hand and secured to a bracelet. This ornament is known as a *kaff* (literally glove).

Rich decoration on tapered shoulders continuing around the shank, was a fashion in rings two thousand years ago. A characteristic of Bedouin finger-rings is the use of elaborate filigree and applied work on both shank and shoulder and this gives them an ornateness similar to that of ancient rings.

Left: It has been claimed that all silver bezelled finger-rings were once the preserve of Bedouin men on the Peninsula. This is borne out by the fact that such rings are still worn by men in the southern regions where modernization has been slower. The thin silver rings without bezels are called marami *and are worn in twos, threes and fours by women today. They are said to have originated in the Wadi Dawasir. The coin and bell ring, often called* mata'hin, *is believed to be from Najran. The date on this coin is obliterated but it can be recognized as one issued in the time of King Abd al Aziz ibn Abd al-Rahman Al Saud, the founder of the Kingdom of Saudi Arabia. With the exception of the coin ring, the silversmithing technique used to decorate these rings is fusing as in granulation. Balls and shapes have been fused to simple shanks.*

93

Frank Cox

Above: *The turquoise rings in this picture represent the range of silver finger-rings with set blue stones. There is a square-shaped turquoise finger-ring but this is more often fashioned in gold and a central hole sometimes displays a gold pin. The mineral, chrysocolla, a copper silicate resembling turquoise, is occasionally seen in these square rings. Turquoise is customarily employed in flat form by the Bedouin jeweller. The rare, slightly domed, or "tallow-topped cabochon" turquoise ring with the brass bezel was crafted in Al Hasa.*

Above *and* right: *The top three turquoise rings are from Hotat Bani Tamim in the Najd, and the thin turquoise ring is also from the Najd. The big rings are worn on the middle fingers and fore-finger. The red stone rings attest to the importance of red as a colour for a set stone in Bedouin rings. Whether garnet or carnelian, top, or a crudely fashioned, roughly set piece of glass in low-grade silver, red is traditional and therefore desired. A red stone ring is often called* fatkhah – *the word for a red gem.* Aqiq ahmar *means semi-precious.*

Frank Cox

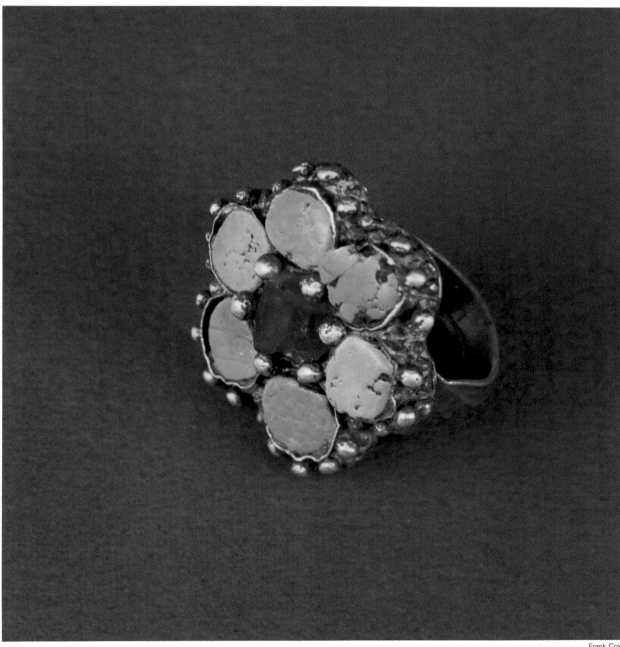

Frank Cox

Left: *This pretty finger-ring resembles a flower – six turquoise "petals" and a red stone "pistil" are accented with a coarse form of granulation commonly employed by the Arabian silversmith. The style is claimed by an area in west-central Arabia known as Hotat Bani Tamim where many large turquoise studded rings have originated. This is the most feminine-looking bezel design amongst the range of women's traditional finger-rings, yet it may not be meant to resemble a flower. The ratio of approximately one red stone to six blue stones can be seen in other Najdi and Northern jewellery. Long ago, this design may have been symbolic. They are becoming increasingly scarce and rarely can anything but a badly damaged example be found for sale in the* souqs. *It is believed that Bedouin women have long since ceased to wear this style in favour of gold rings.*

Right: *Most Bedouin finger-rings are sturdy and solid-looking, even when bells are pendant. Bells are usually an attractive but unimposing addition to the basic ring design. This unusual example seems like a bit of nonsense in comparison. The tiny orange bead perched on top of the larger coral-coloured bead adds to this ring's festive quality. The large silver balls are attached by figure eight links. The shank, shoulders and bezel are decorated with the applied metal-working techniques of filigree and granulation.*

95

Regional Styles

It is certain that Bedouin jewellery made and worn on the Arabian Peninsula once displayed regional characteristics, yet the various sources consulted often provided conflicting details. It is almost impossible to find two people who agree today about what was worn where and when – and upon the names for each ornament. Names for traditional pieces vary tremendously, even within a given region, so only the most commonly employed appellations are provided – and in the dialect used by the informant. An Arabic linguist confirms that dialects of colloquial Arabic are abundant on the Peninsula, and it is therefore virtually impossible to satisfy everyone with the transliterated names. For this reason a full description and classification has been attempted.

As modern transport has displaced many aspects of traditional Arabian life, it is to be expected that giving provenance to Bedouin jewellery is difficult – the art of the silversmith is quite naturally affected as are other facets of the old desert culture. Distinct regional differences in jewellery styles and forms of embellishment did exist prior to the unification of the tribes earlier this century because silversmiths then had limited contact with

people from neighbouring regions. Today, it is not unusual to find a Yemeni silversmith working in Riyadh because he can make more money in Saudi Arabia than he can at home. However, even long ago, the same basic characteristics were shared by Bedouin jewellery from all regions of Arabia and there have always been similarities between the ornaments worn by desert people in Arabia and those in other Middle Eastern countries.

Genevieve Puyraimond, a Central Province resident for over twenty years, believes that awarding provenance to various pieces of jewellery was a difficult task even in the fifties. She can confirm only one style of necklace as unique to the Najd and one as being peculiar to the Hijaz. There are short accounts of traditional jewellery by early travellers and these fortunately throw some light on the subject of regional styles and some jewellery traditions still exist in the southern regions. These seem to parallel what is remembered elsewhere and provide evidence towards a complete picture.

Central

The Najd (Central Arabia) means "highland", referring to the flat plateau that spreads over the central part of the Arabia Peninsula. It sits in geographical isolation and in the past the Najd was inaccessible – flanked to the west by the Sarawat mountain range, while the other three sides are bordered by a desert wilderness. Stark landscapes comprise a large part of the interior but there are occasional springs and wells. The weather is excessively dry and the rainfall is low. Yet the capital city of the Kingdom of Saudi Arabia, situated in the heart of the Najd, is called Riyadh – "the gardens" – referring to a vast oasis of date palms and other vegetation to which, through the centuries, Bedouin from arid outlying areas habitually made their way as summer approached.

In total contrast to the surrounding regions, the Najd, by virtue of its inhospitable and arid perimeter, has had little outside influence in the past and even the most intrepid explorers were usually deterred. Consequently, for thousands of years, artistic expression here was a mere evolution of ancient forms, virtually uninterrupted and unadulterated. This led many Arabists to name the Najd "true Arabia" and it was therefore the most fascinating province for them; Najdis are often referred to as the aristocrats of Arabs. Lady Anne Blunt called this region "the cradle of the Arab race".

There is one particularly beautiful head ornament (*hilyat shaar*) that is said to be peculiar to the Najd. A similar and perhaps identical headpiece

was worn by a woman in Hayil in the late nineteenth century. Hayil, in Jabal Shammar – now considered to be part of northern Arabia – was commonly referred to as the Najd long ago. Many costume and jewellery customs are very similar in both the Najd and Hayil area and the region in between. The *hilyat shaar* in question, is usually made of fine gold and set with matrix turquoise and garnets but is sometimes made in brass with genuine turquoise and red glass. Correctly, it is worn attached to three gold and turquoise *ilagah* that hang pendant behind the head and over each ear although the complete set is difficult to find. Each section is fringed with Gulf pearls and sewn to a red cloth backing. This set and similar gold and turquoise jewellery are an important part of the Najdi range, as are delicate gold and pearl pieces. Old gold and turquoise jewellery and the gold and pearl ornaments present an exception to the traditional Bedouin rule for melting and reworking. It seems that it is sold when the owner dies but the purchaser is reluctant to have the pieces destroyed. Consequently, this jewellery can be quite old. The workmanship is vastly superior on gold ornaments and this is perhaps because they are older and were made at a time when craftsmanship was of a higher standard than today.

Mrs. Puyraimond confirms that one style of necklace featuring colourful coral and agate (real or fake) belongs to the Najd. It has either five or seven round gold (sometimes brass) and turquoise medallion pendants. The oldest versions are said to have had only five pendants and this would

seem to be the correct number, judging by the occasional find of an old necklace that has not been recently rethreaded. Long ago in the Middle East, the numbers five, seven, nine and eleven were considered efficacious in warding off the effects of the Evil Eye. As the silver relief beads in an Arabian Bedouin necklace usually number nine or eleven, it seems likely that threading customs of traditional Arabia are very ancient indeed. Some of the oldest versions of this style of necklace have smaller medallions and consist of a double strand of beads and pendants. It is quite usual to find a few blue beads incorporated and some pear-shaped pendant agates interspersed with coral beads.

There are also twisted Celtic-styled bracelets, sometimes made of pure silver, claimed as Najdi. Heavy twisted metal was popular with both Roman and Celtic jewellers. Chained ornaments, so fashionable in medieval times, are also characteristic of Central Arabian Bedouin jewellery. Early trade with the Romans and later an intercourse with the Crusaders may have been responsible for the transference of these styles to the heartland of Arabia.

Marami, thin silver finger-rings worn in groups of two, three and four are supposed to have originated in the Wadi Dawasir area of the Central Province, although they are also worn today in neighbouring regions to the south-west. The prettiest ring of all, a large bezelled turquoise and red stone design resembling a flower, is said to be traditional in Hotat Bani Tamim, south-west of Riyadh.

Frank Cox

Opposite page: This Najdi necklace has been re-threaded in the traditional style from fine gold and turquoise medallions and an assortment of Najdi beads. It is difficult to find five matching medallions as most of the necklaces have been broken up and the pieces sold separately at a high price. The threading is approximately as shown but the beads can be real coral, agate, gold and turquoise. Just as often they are fake and the quality of gold varies and occasionally the medallions are brass. Old examples sometimes feature seven pendant medallions and the strand is sometimes double.

Left: Fine silver, good stones and excellent workmanship make up this pair of Najdi asawir. The snug-fitting hinge and pin fastening style of bracelet was once made in several qualities but rarely are they seen as beautiful as these. The turquoise and garnet have simple collets with fluted surrounds – the bracelets are chased.

97

Northern

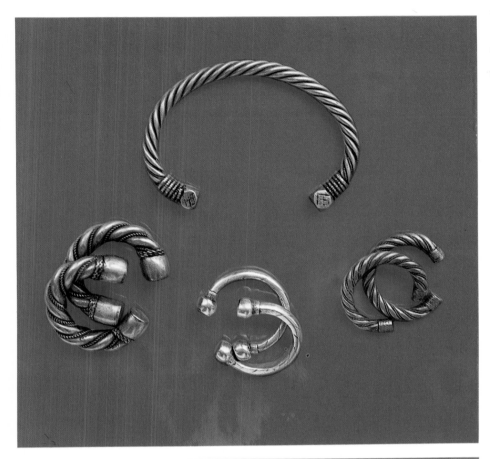

The northern region of Greater Arabia comprises the Nafud desert, the Aja and Salma mountains of Jabal Shammar to the south, and to the north, lava flows – most of which comprise an upland plateau of dark-coloured rock and gravel surfaces that is geographically part of the Syrian desert. There are numerous wadis in this area, and the most significant of these dry river beds is Wadi Sirhan – a large basin set in the surrounding plateau that sprouts sparse grass and steppe vegetation. The climate throughout the northern region is harsh, with extreme heat and a paucity of rain. Temperatures in excess of 120°F are not uncommon.

The greater part of this arid terrain comprises the Northern Province of the Kingdom of Saudi Arabia. The neighbouring countries bordering Saudi Arabia are, from west to east, Jordan, Iraq and Kuwait, and beyond lies Syria and Iran – Persia of old. In the past, the desert people from these lands shared a common way of life. One of the major Arabian tribes, the Rwalla, still traverse a *dirah* (traditional grazing ground) which covers a vast area crossing the Saudi border. It is therefore not surprising that Arabian Bedouin silver jewellery from the northern region of Saudi Arabia is similar to ornaments worn just across the border – and all are similar to jewellery from the ancient civilizations that once thrived in the vicinity.

Torque-like choker necklaces (*kirdala*), supporting multiple pendants of elongated beads, and hoop bracelets featuring bulbous terminals both indicate Persian influence – and these are said to have originated in northern Arabia. Also claimed as northern, is a small silver gem-encrusted triangular *ilagah* overlaid with gold. It has pendant chains that support silver "scarabs" or "pistachios" instead of the more common ball. This motif is seen in jewellery from lands further north and the scarab motif and style of embellishment suggest Egyptian influence.

It can be seen that gemstones most readily available in a region usually appear in the local craftsman's jewellery. In the north turquoise is predominant. The fact that fine turquoise is found on the Sinai Peninsula and in Iran supports the theory that this aspect of regional styles came into existence because of a ready availability of materials. Turquoise is usually found alongside copper which was once mined on the Arabian Peninsula – providing another possible early source of this gemstone. Yet Alois Musil did not mention turquoise as part of a Rwalla woman's jewellery in the nineteenth century. According to Musil, each woman wore approximately the same pieces and these featured coral, copper, brass, silver, glass and "glass pearls".

Traditional Rwalla jewellery included a coral necklace (*mahnaka*), a glass pearl necklace (*zelade*), a finger-ring (*fatha*), small black glass bangles (*sbat*), small black glass armlets (*ma'azed*), a copper nose-ring worn in the right nostril (*zmam*), copper ear-rings (*turzijjl*), brass or silver ring, two–five cms. in diameter, and worn in the left nostril (*zmejjem*) and glass or copper finger-rings (*hgul*) to match the bangles and ear-rings. Lady Anne Blunt and Ger-

Above: *Dozens of twisted bracelets resembling ancient Celtic ornaments are sold in the Najd. They are solid and the thickest of them is extremely heavy and hard-wearing. The quality of silver varies tremendously and on occasions there is a copper core. The central pair are the finest silver and the roundness of the rods has worn down considerably due to the inherent softness. The torque is rarely seen and this one was purchased in Yemen. Similar torque necklaces are worn by Bedouin women in Afghanistan. That Bedouin jewellery is the personal wealth of a woman who may sell it at will probably accounts for the occasional piece of this design being found great distances apart. It is known that the Najd and Northern Arabia share many costume customs, so the prevalence of this style in the Najd where the biggest trade in Bedouin jewellery exists – and the Afghanistan connection – possibly makes this style one shared between the central and northern regions.*

Above: *Occasionally a bracelet of this design is found in the Riyadh souq. It is virtually impossible to find a matched pair. Most are badly damaged. The style is said to be from the north and this is acceptable when the design is compared with the traditional pieces worn by tribal women living in Afghanistan, Iraq and northern Iran – their silver jewellery traditions are similar to those of the*

Peninsula. Pilgrims travelling to Mecca from Afghanistan sell some jewellery each year, and this can usually be recognized by the set stones. For example, the blue stones are usually lapis lazuli and red stones are garnet or fine carnelian. Perhaps this broad bracelet comes from a land beyond the Euphrates. Bedouin traders insist it is from the Arabian Peninsula.

trude Bell do mention more elaborate jewellery and this is probably because they visited the *hareems* of well-to-do settled desert women. Gertrude Bell was met at Hayil by a woman wearing "a rope of bright pearls". Lady Anne Blunt spent an afternoon with ladies who wore intricate head ornaments of gold and turquoise; the various plate-like pieces were connected to each other by chains and all ornaments were trimmed with pearls. Nose-rings of gold, pearl and turquoise were also chained to the complete headgear. She also noted that the poorer Bedouin women wore silver ornaments. Coral is also mentioned.

Above: Multiple pendants are characteristic of Arabian Bedouin jewellery. The fringes are commonly chain and invariably they support balls, bells or charms. This choker style of necklace, claimed as Northern, was found in the Najd. It is known as a kirdala. The figure eight links between the choker band and the elongated bead, and between this bead

and the balls, is found on jewellery in other parts of the Peninsula too. The styling seems Persian. The influence of Persia was given opportunity to spread after the conquest by Alexander the Great around 330 BC. Persian artistic vitality has seen expression again and again down through the ages and may well have recurred here in this piece on the

Arabian Peninsula. It is a traditional style and there is no way of knowing exactly when and where it originated. The choker band is decorated with filigree and coarse granulation, and tiny collets house red and blue stones. While the basic shape is always the same, this embellishment varies according to the talents and desires of the silversmith.

Eastern

The Eastern Province of the Kingdom of Saudi Arabia was once known as Al Hasa – referring to the murmuring sound coming from the welcoming waters of the Hofuf oasis. Hofuf, a town of considerable size and an important trading centre, was the former capital of this region. This Province comprises sandy shores and salt flats, the drifting sands of the Dahna desert, a rock plateau called the Summan and a section of the great southern desert, the Rub al-Khali (also known as the Empty Quarter). Eastern Arabia was once famous for fabulous pearls but now it is known primarily for oil. In fact, the other countries located in the eastern portion of the Arabian Peninsula are also famous world-wide because of oil. They are generally referred to as the peripheral states (of the Arabian Peninsula) and comprise Kuwait, Bahrain, Qatar and the seven United Arab Emirates: Abu Dhabi, Dubai, Sharjah, Ajman, Umm al-Qaiwain, Ras al-Khaimah and Fujairah. Trucial Oman (the tip of the Musandam Peninsula) is logically included in this eastern portion as it shares a similar geography and history, as does one other segment of the Sultanate of Oman, and that is the Muscat coastal area.

In the fifth century AD north-eastern Arabia came under Persian influence, but even before this, the influence of Persia was cast over the entire eastern area because Arabs and Persians interacted in the Gulf area. The eastern portion of the Peninsula has been subject to continual foreign favoured Roman style. Matched pairs of hollow hoop bracelets with pebbles trapped in hollow terminals are worn there also. These are reminiscent of Oriental bracelets, and Persian in particular.

The crescent-moon shape is somewhat more prevalent as a jewellery component in the eastern parts of the Peninsula. Perhaps this is because of the Ottoman occupation from 1871 until 1913; the crescent is an ancient shape which gathered new meaning with the Ottoman Empire. During Ottoman rule it was adopted as a Muslim sign and today it is seen above mosques all over the world. It is also worn in India as a jewellery component. Although claimed that India inherited the shape from Persia much earlier, it is likely the crescent as a jewellery shape, reached there with the Muslim Mughals – at least the shape would have been popularized during the dynasty as they were inordinately fond of jewellery.

H.R.P. Dickson took note of Bedouin jewellery worn in Kuwait and eastern regions of Arabia early this century. A great deal of the jewellery listed is gold, studded with turquoise – pearls are also prevalent. The ornaments are in striking contrast to jewellery inventories for Northern Arabia where glass and copper predominates. Colonel Dickson does remark that townswomen wore more gold than the nomadic women; while the latter seemed to prefer silver, it may have been a matter of wealth or belief.

Frank Cox

Above: *Children in the eastern portion of the Peninsula, particularly towards the south, wear belled anklets which were believed to be amuletic.*

Above: *Trapped pebbles rattle in snake-like coil bracelets once worn in central and eastern Arabia. The technique of chasing decorates this fine silver.*

Frank Cox

influences because of the access afforded by the Gulf. Pirates and traders of several nationalities used this waterway from earliest time. One bulbous-beaded hoop ear-ring, claimed to be typical of the Eastern province, suggests an origin in ancient Assyria and the heavy spiked bracelets and anklets also found there resemble African jewellery. The latter style probably arrived by way of trading ships that entered the Gulf.

An unusual cabochon-shaped turquoise mounted in a brass and silver finger-ring is claimed as a style typical of the region, and specifically the Al Hasa area. This ring echoes a

Dickson lists large amber bead bracelets (*khasir*), a colourful fixed bead bracelet (*dalag*), red coral bracelets (*mirjan*), a collar of small coloured beads with five central chain metal drops (*ma'ainna*) and a gold medallion set with turquoise (*zarar*). Another necklace has gold coins of varying size (*sankh* or *khashil*), and there are gold nose-rings – sometimes silver – with two pearls and two turquoise (*fraida*), massive anklets of gold or silver (*hijjil*), plain straight gold bangles (*mathayid*) and a wavy design variation (*mathayid al haiya*), and a gold waistband (*hazzam*) – for the frock (*dara'ah*). The head ornament (*hama*), is a gold cap from which chains (*tallal*) hang down either side of the face. This piece of jewellery is generally reserved for brides, as is the *gub-gub* – another style of golden cap – although the latter is worn also by girls in Kuwait on festive days. The *gub-gub* is fashioned from small joined squares of solid gold – each square being studded with a single turquoise. The *gub-gub* is kept in place by the hair which is threaded through loops at the back and then braided. Also threaded into the hair are *kitbat* – gold drop-like ornaments that hang on strings woven into the plaits of hair at the back of the head. *Kitbat*, he writes, are worn only by the well-to-do. Perhaps these ornaments were not always solid gold; several examples found today that appear to be quite old are made of some lesser metal and there are traces of gold indicating that the ornament has been dipped. So far as it is known, dipping low-grade metal jewellery in precious metals is a very recent practice in Arabia. It is possible that it was practised in eastern Arabia in the past.

As the British political agent based in Kuwait, Dickson worked in the eastern regions of the Arabian peninsula at a time when it was still possible, not only to see regional differences, but also to note tribal fashions in jewellery. The *zarar*, he noted, was common to the Muntafiq tribal women, while the *ma'ainna* was popular with women of the Ajman, Mutair and Dhafir tribes. The latter preferred coral ornaments and nomads generally favoured large-sized nose-rings.

Above: *Thin, hollow bangles have been formed by embossing. Applied shapes and fine filigree cover the surfaces. The terminal ends are embossed domes and these are overlaid by a diamond-shaped plate. They appear to be quite new but the style is old. Spiky protusions such as these are believed to be typical of old bangles from Al Hasa, or the Eastern Province.*

Left: *The* gub-gub *is recorded by Colonel Dickson as a gold head ornament peculiar to the eastern regions of the Peninsula. The pendant discs are worn hanging over the forehead, and tresses at the back of the head are threaded through the rings. This old* gub-gub *has been worn as a necklace and it appears to have been gold-plated. Turquoise was set in the gold examples recorded by Dickson. The section which rests on the top of the head is formed from hinged segments. The chain has been added by the last owner and not the trader. It was sold thus to the* souq *by Bedouin.*

101

Western

Hijaz is the name traditionally applied to the western province of the Kingdom of Saudi Arabia – the region adjacent to the Red Sea and including the port of Jeddah and the holy cities of Mecca and Medina.

The word Hijaz means barrier, referring to the great escarpment that runs from north to south forming a natural corridor – the path used by ancient frankincense and myrrh traders from the south.

In every respect, the Hijaz is a region of great variety, there are vast dry deserts and lush cultivated areas. At the highest point, over 1,800 metres above sea level, stands Tayif, the traditional summer place of rich townspeople – the area famous for fruit and flowers, and the home of strong traditions where many of Arabia's finest handicrafts are produced. Southward, toward the coast, lies the Tihama, or lowland area. Here, as in the Asir littoral, Africans have merged with the Arabian population, welding their colourful craft techniques to those of traditional Arabia.

Western Arabia is the most cosmopolitan province because it has been exposed to so many different influences throughout the centuries. The Red Sea was always a thriving waterway, despite hazardous currents, and trading ships went back and forth to various ports, stopping at Jeddah. There is also the annual flow of pilgrims to Mecca and many *Hajis* have settled in the region.

Bedouin jewellery found in western Arabia is quite different to that from the other regions and it sometimes clearly reflects some influences that can be traced. Mrs. Puyraimond confirms that one style of pendant medallion necklace once came only from Tayif. A similar medallion decorates some bracelets and this perhaps suggests that they, too, are from the Western Province. A medallion is a simple circular pendant that has been universally popular throughout centuries and silversmiths in various parts of the Arabian Peninsula were perhaps once known for specific styles of embellishment.

The largest of silver beads found so far were purchased in the Hijaz. The necklace could have been made outside the Peninsula, of course, but large silver beads appear quite frequently in this region. The evidence so far suggests these large silver beads are more characteristic of jewellery worn in the three regions along the west coast of the Arabian Peninsula than elsewhere.

Motoko Katakura reveals that some tribal women of the Hijaz wear their treasure of silver on their masks. Although silver jewellery is still worn by many Hijazi Bedouin women, it appears that traditional ornaments are worn less and less. Great quantities of Bedouin jewellery are found for sale in the Jeddah *souq*. An elaborate face mask (*burga*) which displays all kinds of silver coins can also be bought secondhand in Jeddah.

Second-hand silver shops sometimes have a style of multi-pendanted necklace that is unique to

Left: *Dozens of pairs of this style of bracelet which are made in Jeddah are eagerly purchased by Westerners. Occasionally a very old pair is found which suggests that the style is traditional. Whether they are actually Arabian or an imported style is not known. Although silver, these wrought hoops seem alien amongst the broad range of traditional styles.*
Right: *The fish motif is quite prevalent in the Hijaz and it is also seen in the neighbouring lands to the north of the Peninsula. This Hijazi purchase has pendant discs and links of foreign make. The stones are red.*

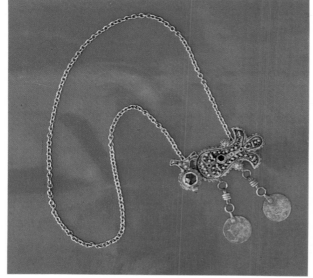

Right: *Embossing and repoussé chasing decorate these hollow horseshoe bracelets. The set stones are red, blue and green. Green stones are not common on the Peninsula and they are never seen in the heartland. They are found quite often in the Hijaz and may be due to influence of neighbouring lands or the jewellery may have come from outside.*

the Hijaz. Some examples are still strung on the original cotton threading and there have been sufficient available to confirm correct bead placement. A large bulbar-shaped central pendant set with red and blue beads divides a strand of hollow silver fish (*samak*) that are threaded through their heads. Tiny charms (*hijab*) swing from their tails. The fish is an ancient motif and has long been a symbol of life and fecundity in the Middle East. It is still a common jewellery motif in the lands just over the northern borders of the Kingdom of Saudi Arabia, while it is not made now on the Peninsula. Women now buy modern gold jewellery which

does not include this motif. The fish necklace also features one blue and several green beads amongst spherical dividing silver beads.

Red and blue stones are commonly set in Western Arabian Bedouin jewellery, just as they are in the other parts of the Peninsula. Additionally, green and white stones are found in traditional Hijazi ornaments. Green and white stones are prevalent in Syrian and Jordanian Bedouin jewellery, so it seems the influence from these neighbouring lands has had some effect. Some of the jewellery with green and white stones found in the *souq* may have been made in Syria and Jordan and

entered the Kingdom of Saudi Arabia with its wearer. Some ornaments have been definitely identified as Bedouin jewellery from these and other Middle Eastern countries. The pieces are said to have been sold during the period of *Haj*, when the woman was in need of additional funds. Very recently, the traders of the Riyadh Women's *souq* have actively sought wares from near and far and this represents the beginnings of a "tourist" trade. Prior to this, items sold in the *souq* were available only in the traditional course of events. It is the demand of the Western buyer that has brought forth the supply.

Above: *Original threading is secured by a loop over a green bead on this western Arabian necklace. The hollow silver fish, once a sign of fertility, are strung by their heads and hijab swing from their tails. One blue bead, quite likely to avert the Evil Eye in times past, vies with a majority of silver beads and five green beads.*

South-western and Southern

South of the Hijaz, or western Arabia, lies the Asir – the south-western region of the Kingdom of Saudi Arabia. Asir means "difficult region", and refers to terrain that comprises high peaks, deep terraced valleys, plateaux over 1,200 metres high and coastal lowland. From the northern-most point of the Asir's Sarawat mountain range, the land eastward slopes gently down to the Rub al-Khali – the largest sandy desert in Arabia. Westward, the Tihama – a lowland strip of sandy plain and scrubby valleys – is bordered on one side by the mountains and on the other by the Red Sea.

Directly beyond the formidable Rub al-Khali are three other countries which are, from west to east, the two Yemens: Yemen Arab Republic (Y.A.R.), the People's Democratic Republic of Yemen (P.D.R.Y.) and the Sultanate of Oman. These lands form part of traditional Arabia, sharing many of the same age-old environmental problems as well as a common cultural heritage and the unifying religion of Islam.

North Yemen (Y.A.R.) is divided into two distinct geographical areas: a flat coastal plain of sand dunes and scrub with an occasional oasis and an interior mountain region with jagged peaks rising up to approximately 3,400 metres – and, cradled in the mountains, there is a large central plain of rich volcanic soil. While the shore plains of the Tihama suffer a harsh desert climate, the arable mountain regions are temperate with abundant rain.

South Yemen (P.D.R.Y.) sits at the southern end of the Arabian plateau; the land comprises ancient granites partly covered by sedimentary limestone and sand, and a narrow flat coastal area. Further inland, the country is mountainous, reaching a height of approximately 1,800 metres in the west and tapering off to the east. The tableland is interspersed with arid valleys and wadis. Eastward – located in the central part of the country and running parallel to the coast – lies the legendary Wadi Hadramaut, a name that many translate as "death is present". This narrow, mostly arid valley is surrounded by desolate hills and desert. South Yemen suffers high temperatures, especially along the coast, and droughts are common; coastal humidity and dust storms in the interior afford little relief.

The Sultanate of Oman occupies the south-east corner of the Arabian Peninsula. Geographically, Oman is divided by natural features into several distinct districts: the tip of the Musandam Peninsula and the Muscat-Matrah coastal area (which, so far as regional differences are concerned, relate more to the eastern portion of Arabia than to the south), and "Inner Oman" comprising the Jabal Akdar or Green Mountain, the western foothills and the desert fringes, the southern Province of Dhofar and the offshore island of Masirah. Except for Dhofar, where it is green and there are perennial streams, the black volcanic rock and creamy gravel plains of Oman present a formidable land where the summer climate is one of the hottest in

Left: *Repoussé chasing is usual for this style of southern bracelet or anklet. The anklet would have a hinged opening and pinned fastening, and there would be a "safety" chain attached to the pin. This example has lost its matched pair and was in a sad condition until burnished with a brush with brass bristles. Several silver balls are missing.*

Above: *A floral design is surrounded by geometric patterns on this charm case from Oman. Rough chasing is most effective on this purse-shaped receptacle. The top opens and it may have been designed to hold a tiny Koran or koranic verses. The delicate chain fringe does not resemble the support chain which may not be original.*

the world. Inner Oman is an isolated place, hemmed in by the sea on one side and by the desert vastness of the Rub al-Khali on the other; the Hajar mountain chain also forms a natural barrier between the coast and desert from the Musandam Promontory to the city of Sur.

Generally, in southern Arabia, it is easy to study the past because changes have been less sweeping and traditional lifestyles, therefore, have been less affected than in the Kingdom of Saudi Arabia and the Emirates. In Oman, in particular, remarkably primitive jewellery still exists and it casts interesting light upon the total picture of Bedouin jewellery. For instance, objects such as dried seed pods, pieces of wood, bone, stone, teeth and even a jawbone of a fox can still be found set in fine silver. Necklaces from the Interior are often festooned with talismans such as these and they are worn for the purpose of protecting the wearer. Unlike jewellery from any other part of the Peninsula, a dress pendant can be of camel bone rather than metal. Also, representations of the human form (either as a small charm or as an engraving on a medallion) are worn by women to avert evil and to aid them in childbirth. Particular shapes of beads in Oman are also believed to help and give protection from special illnesses. The snake shape is said to be especially protective. Silver itself was apparently once worn in the belief that it was a powerful agent against the evil eye.

A wealth of fabulous Bedouin jewellery styles is accredited to south-western and southern Arabia. In fact, the silversmiths from these regions have a reputation so great that the Riyadh Women's *souq* traders automatically say that a fine ornament is from the south when they actually have no idea of its origin.

Leather ornaments studded with silver are characteristic of the south-west and many such pieces are still worn by men there. Bells and belled ornaments are said to have originated in the south, specifically in Najran, and the belled and meshed style of hinged-opening, pin fastening anklet, bracelet and belt set are attributed to these regions. Elaborate meshed collars (*kirdan*) that resemble chain mail, are also claimed by the south.

There are differences between the jewellery worn to the west, in Yemen, and that worn to the east, in Oman. Sylvia Kennedy writes of a multi-stranded coral and silver ceremonial necklace that was traditionally worn by a Yemeni woman on two occasions in her life – at the time of her marriage and upon motherhood. (Yemeni brides today do not yearn for coral and silver and look to gold for dowry.) On both of these momentous occasions, she would be elaborately dressed and sit in state wearing the special necklace, *iqd mirjan*. All other jewellery worn at these times could be used on other occasions, but the *iqd mirjan* was added only on the first and second days of her wedding celebration, and whenever she received female guests during her forty days of confinement after

Left; *This rectangular charm case pendant is typical of Omani work. The piece is finely crafted and the silver is good. Repoussé chasing decorates the face of the* hirz *and the pendant charms are accented with applied filigree. These charms are the two-fingered version of the hand of Fatimah, a popular shape with Bedouin jewellery makers. This style of chain is not the most common. It is rarely seen on the Peninsula and would seem to be a result of outside influence. The small pendant charms,* hijab *are usually mere rough-cut bits of metal attached to links.*

the examples for sale today are poor an obviously rethreaded. Yet, true to Arabian custom, the traditional style is more important than the quality. The coral beads in an *iqd mirjan* are more or less uniform in size but the bead size varies from necklace to necklace as does the quality of coral – and fakes are common. The silver also varies in fineness. The largest, smoothest and darkest coral beads are the most expensive and are often seen with the smooth and glowing patina of fine silver.

Small beads are actually preferred as more strands are then possible – twelve to fourteen strands are not uncommon. Each strand of coral is generally interspersed with silver beads of a specific style which have special names. The largest central bead (*heikal*) is in fact a sealed, cylindrical, round-ended charm case and sometimes supports pendants – usually charms, balls or coins. Each side of the *heikal* is met with a silver spherical bead (*jauz*), and this style of bead appears again half way up each side of the strands, with a further *jauz* at each end of the strands before the mace-shaped terminal bead (*mizmar*). There is usually another small five-sided silver bead (*tut*) – constructed of clustered "mulberry" spheres and these appear interspersed with the coral in no specific order. All the other beads are traditionally formed by filigree and are very finely crafted. Old Yemeni medallions are often formed from filigree. Most Yemeni charm cases and medallions are now created from flat metal and the surfaces are embellished with granulation and applied filigree instead.

The set stones in Yemeni jewellery are beautiful and interesting. It is claimed that turquoise and garnet are found in the south-west, yet, carnelian is the chosen stone. In fact, Yemeni carnelian has been prized for centuries and superb examples are still found in jewellery and daggers. Coral is commonly added to most necklaces as a bead and it is sometimes threaded through pendant chains that hang from charm cases. This is not only attractive, but it holds the ends of long pendants fairly rigid when the threading appears at the bottom of them. Sometimes this threaded line of coral beads appears at the top and bottom of the chain pendants. large cube-shaped amber beads (both real and fake) are also commonly worn, particularly near the coast.

Silver predominates as the metal for jewellery but gold is worn. Ibri women in Oman can be seen wearing a spectacular golden head circlet over a sombre black headcloth. *Hirz* necklaces in Dhofar and along the Muscat coast are often gold. Rijal, in the south-west, is one of several places that were once famous for goldsmithing.

Omani jewellery is especially notable as it is generally of the finest silver and workmanship. Charm cases in particular display superior workmanship and often open on hinges, whereas charm cases elsewhere on the Peninsula are usually sealed. Jewellery embellishment in Oman relies on metal-working techniques such as chasing and engraving rather than set stones, filigree and granulation.

Top: *Worn as armlets or anklets, these heavy silver ornaments are cumbersome. This style has been seen for sale in Riyadh consistently over ten years and they are claimed as anklets. It is possible that they were once worn by men as armlets as they fit quite well on the bare arm of a man. It is unlikely that a woman would wear them thus. They seem African in appearance.*

Above: *Southern Arabia yields some Bedouin pieces which suggest influence from neighbouring Africa or nearby India. These "slave" bracelets are said to be Arabian but display Indian* coins and characteristics of *Indian tribal jewellery. For centuries the west coast of India has reflected Arabian jewellery-making techniques while Arabian pieces can seem Indian.*

giving birth. If she did not own such a necklace, it was usually borrowed or rented from professional women who, by custom, groom brides throughout the Peninsula.

According to Sylvia Kennedy, *iqd mirjan* have not been made for over thirty years, and, in fact,

There are differences to be seen in jewellery-making techniques, too, and the most obvious involves gold. Apparently gold is overlaid on silver in the most interesting fashion – much as it was done long ago in Europe. Gold coins are hammered onto a silver base or a thin gold sheet is "sweated" on. Engraving cuts away the gold to reveal silver. According to Ruth Hawley, an authority on Omani Bedouin jewellery, this work is prevalent in Sur and the Sharqiyah. Another interesting jewellery-making technique, unknown in Saudi Arabia, requires the decorated silver to be blackened with soot and oil or sulphur. A final polish brightens the relief, leaving the background dark for contrast. Similar work is done in Iran.

Silver for Omani jewellery is said to be imported in bar form today, from China. According to National Geographic, gold in bar form comes from places northward. Long ago, it is likely that precious metals were mined locally. Ruth Hawley has written that the head of many Bedouin families attaches his wealth to the wrists, ankles and neck of his wife. For her, the jewellery perhaps represents an appreciative husband; she is, for him, a walking bank acount most certainly and possibly a source of prestige.

The styles of jewellery in Oman are many and varied and Ruth Hawley believes this could be the result of itinerant jewellers following fortune and introducing new designs. This may have happened long ago, as it is also acknowledged that

indigenous jewellers are generally loathe to change traditional styles to any great extent. It is likely that the styles are ancient and evolved very slowly.

Although it is difficult today to award provenance to pieces, Mrs. Hawley has noted that set stones, while rare, are more typical of Muscat, Matrah and the Batinah coast. Generally, coral and imitation coral are strung with silver and gold beads wherever coloured beads are worn. Coral is also mounted in ear-rings and on necklace components. Plastic and glass are used also, particularly as set components. Beads of materials other than silver and coral are more characteristic of Dhofari jewellery which is thought to have been subject to African influence.

Dhofari jewellery, according to Ruth Hawley, relates more to Yemeni styles than to that worn in the rest of Oman: "It is generally more solid". Silverwork has all but ceased in Dhofar except for the production of hair pendants. These cone-shaped pieces (athgeel – singular: athgul) are worn ten at a time, hanging on wool at the back of the head. They are filled with scented wool or cloth. Chains (silsila) are popular and one style (manjad), worn around the neck and under one arm, is hidden under the woman's clothes. It is thought to be associated with fertility. Also typical of Dhofar, is a shoulder brooch (sils), which is a triangular piece with pendants that often incorporate a charm in the shape of the human form. This is believed to

Left: *Rectangular charm cases from southern regions vary in that those from the eastern side are usually chased silver and the ones from the western side have applied embellishment and set red stones. The red stones are semi-precious, fake, or ceramic beads. Fine cabochon carnelians, for which Yemen is famous, are found on these* hirz, *see* top left *and* top right. *The shape of these* hirz *is stressed with beaded wire, filigree and lines of fused-on spheres, discs and diamonds. The alloyed silver is sturdy and most of these sealed charm cases are undamaged. Some fine silver* hirz *are padded with wadding or wood to save the soft metal box from dents. Apart from embellishment, rectangular charm cases from all southern regions are similar. They support a fringe on the bottom edge which is formed from chain or figure eight links which have silver balls pendant. Small charms of various shapes, particularly the hand of Fatimah, are often included.*

Above: *An elaborate meshed collar of this style is known as* kirdan. *The variants exhibit few ornamental differences – they are usually just varying lengths. The longest can extend from the neck to the waistline. This is one of the shortest. It is a particularly fine example because there are funnel-shaped terminal beads and these are connected to a fine silver plaited rope. White cotton is threaded through the necklace at two levels, in and out of links. This is a common practice, particularly on pendant fringes and coral beads are sometimes added to this kind of threadwork. The* kirdan *is often backed with cotton which may also be designed to support the piece. The silversmith who designed the original* kirdan *may have been inspired by the armour of the Crusaders as this intricate meshwork definitely resembles chain mail. It is believed that Arabian warriors saw or fought in chain mail suits as some ancient metal garments can be found in the antique* souq *in Riyadh.*

be a fertility symbol, too. The ornament resembles an *ilagah* and, in fact, it is worn as a headdress pendant sometimes.

Married women and girls in Dhofar wear caps (*harus*) with silver cylindrical pendant beads and coins stitched to them. Married women have ten beads while single girls wear six – divided equally at each side of the face. Dhofari ear-rings are usually large hoops with conical beads forming part of the ring. The *malnaut* bracelet, commonly seen, is made up of faceted solid silver beads interspersed with real or fake cylindrical coral beads and groups of five thin serrated-edged beads – the whole repeated four times. The *mhadabit* is a traditional "D"-shaped bracelet with alternate filigree and projections on the flat side while the curved side is the "Celtic" twist seen in Central Arabian bracelets. The *malnaut* and *mhadabit* are customarily worn together. Dhofari anklets are usually wide bands of elaborate chain work fringed with bells.

Jewellery embellishment was once clearly distinctive in each region of Oman. Although jewellery is more mobile today, there is sufficient evidence to draw some conclusions. For instance, circles as decoration seem to predominate around Sur, while ornaments with projections predominate in Muscat, Matrah and the Batinah coastal area. Heavy anklets (*natal* or *ental*) are typical of Nizwa and Rostag. According to Ruth Hawley, these may be called *hajil*. They are apparently given sometimes by a father to his daughter at puberty.

Above: *This southern necklace is not very old and seems to be a derivative of the* iqd mirjan, *a traditional Yemeni necklace which features multi-stranded corals between silver beads – the bottom bead an elongated cylinder. A cylindrical amulet case such as the one here is usually known as a* khiyarah *but the counterpart on an* iqd mirjan *is called* heikal. *The* heikal *is sealed but this charm case opens.*

Many children throughout the Omani Interior wear flat anklets and some are decorated with bells – these are known as *hawajil*. Another twisted silver style with a pin fastening is called *weil*. Omani girls, especially in the Interior, braid their hair into elaborate circular ornaments with pendants. The hair is divided into ten plaits which are braided half way down at the back into a horizontal plait of goat hair. The ornament is fixed into this. Ornate headpieces are usually worn on the forehead and are generally reserved for weddings. Around Rostag, a silver coin is commonly seen hanging on the forehead – this is attached by chain to the headgear.

Omani bracelets are distinctive. The "D" shape is prevalent and the flat side is worn uppermost and encompasses the pinned opening. They are chunky in appearance, particularly in Nizwa.

Intact Omani necklaces are generally threaded on cotton rope and secured by a loop over a rope ball button. The *shabka* necklace, on the other hand, has a wide, flat silver band at the back of the neck which fastens with a hook – or it is held by a chain at the back. It is similar to a northern necklace when it has pendants, but when it is plain, it is more like a Central Arabian torque style. In fact, it is sometimes called *tawq* in the Interior and Sharqiyah. In Rostag, it is known as *shabka*.

Above: *Multi-stranded Arabian necklaces can be pearls, coral, or fake coral. The necklace above displays small silver beads amongst fake coral and the ten sections are divided by ornate silver beads created fom two embossed halves that have been encrusted with silver granules and beaded wire. The matching* hirz *displays the same techniques but the granules are formed into triangles.*

109

The Art of Bedouin Jewellery

Techniques

The basic techniques silversmiths use for fashioning Bedouin jewellery have changed very little since ancient times. Mass production methods, in fact, could not successfully copy most pieces of bedouin jewellery because many of the embellishment techniques involved can be achieved only by the skilled hands of the craftsman. It is a delightful surprise to find these ornaments in an age when handmade items are rare and sought after.

Desert women long ago probably favoured old styles of jewellery at first because they were accustomed to them and the designs were later perpetuated because the ornaments became a tradition. Workmanship naturally varied from smith to smith, but the silver content, as a general rule, was higher than it is in pieces made today and fake gems were less common because jewellery was a currency. For the Bedouin woman in the past, traditional jewellery was not only valuable, it was also useful and decorative. However, it was a custom to provide a proportion of cheaper jewellery in identical traditional designs for those who could not afford the higher prices.

Whatever the metal content, the techniques employed for fashioning Bedouin jewellery are the same. Annealing and hammering are the initial processes, followed by cutting in preparation for embossing, repoussé, chasing and engraving – all methods of giving relief to flat surfaces. The ornamental techniques of filigree and granulation add yet another dimension. Even-gauge wire is produced for making chains. Wrought, cast, fused and soldered metal are also part of jewellery-making tradition. A combination of all these techniques may be employed to produce an elaborate ornament, but sometimes only one decorative technique is used, liberally, to create an exotic effect. All of these processes are followed by the mundane task of "pickling" which is the term used for the final cleansing.

The Bedouin silversmith is usually born into the artisan class. His craft is generally passed on to him by his father who instructs him in traditional techniques and encourages him to produce the styles favoured in his area.

Silversmiths on the Arabian Peninsula are mostly settled or semi-settled folk concentrated in oases and coastal towns. They occasionally become nomadic through affiliation with a large tribe to whose needs they cater for an indefinite period. Often drawn from a town, this silversmith (*sayegh al fiddah*) becomes part of the tribal structure, although he is considered ignoble because of his artisan status.

The settled silversmiths are generally found working close to the *souqs*, where they sit cross-legged, singly or in small groups, tapping out their silver on anvils. They are often bare to the waist because the heat of the desert is intensified by the fires over which they work.

Jewellery is usually made to order, although silversmiths may produce pieces in advance of a sale if they have time. New jewellery is generally sold by weight, the price being fixed according to the silver content and the stones used in the settings.

Traditional styles were once favoured by both the jeweller and customer but occasionally an item of Bedouin jewellery displays originality – one example is the pistachio nut-shaped pendant. Such an unusual ornament must have been an idea conceived by an individualistic craftsman, as most of the jewellery is usually characterized by sym-

Above: *Where does the silver come from? Today, the silver to make Bedouin jewellery in Arabia comes from the bank – in bars. Long ago, locally-mined silver probably sufficed to supplement the silver obtained from melting down old ornaments. Old jewellery is still melted down but it is scarce due to its popularity with Western people in Arabia. The silversmith was once reluctant to sell any of his old stock because he needed the silver. A buyer of second-hand Bedouin jewellery had to go to the women traders. Now he will part with pieces if the price is high enough – he can go to the bank with the good feeling that he has gained in the transaction. He has yet to make this silver into jewellery. The price will be high and unfortunately the work is rarely as fine as it used to be.*

bolic and geometrical shapes with floral and abstract geometical designs. The fish, (samak), is an exception.

The metal-working trades have been severely harmed by competition from imports and the rising costs of labour and materials in recent years. Many craftsmen have gradually been forced into performing metal repairwork. Others are retiring and potential craftsmen are turning to more profitable occupations. As a result, some traditional styles of jewellery are becoming increasingly rare. Many Bedouin are being absorbed into new industries created by the present economic boom and the younger generation is leaving the desert for opportunities in the cities. The inevitable result of these planned or impulsive changes in Bedouin lifestyle is that the long, low, black tents glimpsed between the dunes will soon vanish like a mirage, along with the inhabitants' colourful way of life. Also lost will be the spectacular costumes and beautiful silver jewellery.

In the days before the craftsman melted down jewellery or could buy silver from a town, it was necessary for him to refine precious metal and there is reason to believe that much of it was mined locally. Gold and silver of any sizeable quantity are rarely found in their pure state. As a rule tons of rock must be crushed to yield small nuggets. [Gold is also recovered in minute particles from alluvial beds by painstaking methods although this is not applicable to the Peninsula]. Intense heat must then be applied to melt the tiny pieces into a workable lump.

At some time in the distant past it must have become apparent to the craftsman that the soft, yielding qualities of gold lessened with continual hammering and that reheating the metal returned it to the malleable and ductile medium he desired. This process, known as annealing, was a major technical advance in the ancient world. Annealing (tahmiyah) is the first step in fashioning metal into jewellery. It consists of heating and gradually cooling the metal. This process softens, removes brittleness and makes it malleable for working into shapes or hammering flat into sheets. Many metal products are quenched in water as part of the annealing process, but this method is considered too drastic for jewellery as it leaves fine work brittle. Instead, slow, natural cooling on stone is preferred.

The silver used by the Bedouin silversmith is generally alloyed with base metal but occasionally pure and precious silver and gold ornaments are made. The most common base metal used to alloy silver and gold is copper, for it gives both the required durability and the best sheen. However, tin, zinc and nickel are commonly added.

Before being fashioned into jewellery, silver must be worked up into sheets or wire – unless it is to be used for casting. Most of the silver used in the production of Bedouin jewellery is made into sheets. Some Bedouin buttons are created from sheets of beaten gold folded over a packing agent, such as wood, but non-cast silver ornaments are generally fashioned from thicker sheets than gold so it does not need packing to resist damage. despite this, many lovely pieces of fine old Bedouin silver jewellery have become damaged be-

cause the metal employed was too thin or the object was almost pure silver – the amount of base metal in the alloy being inadequate to withstand wear and tear.

Tiny geometrical shapes (triangles, diamonds and circles), cut out of very thin sheet silver or beaten from tiny silver spheres, often provide relief decoration. these minute shapes are affixed to larger, thicker, geometrical beaten-silver components and other jewellery. The moon shapes (full, half and crescent) are popular – the crescent usually being an inverted component of an ornament. The shape of a jewellery component is usually accented with filigreed silver wire and granulated silver spheres, often called shot. "Moon" pendants are generally embellished with pendant silver balls on the inside as well as on the outside edge.

Silver beads are commonly incorporated into Bedouin necklaces as the largest beads on a strand,

placed at regular intervals for relief. Bead shapes range from annular, bulbar, cylindrical to spherical. Additionally, two mace-shaped silver beads appear on most necklaces in terminal position. Such beads are fashioned from pieces of metal folded cone fashion and then the large end is capped by an embossed dome or finial. Many small silver beads are made of folded metal, too. Generally, Bedouin silver beads (which sometimes measure up to ten centimetres in diameter), are constructed in two halves by the embossing technique.

Obviously the silversmith requires a great deal of sheet metal to make jewellery and much of his time is devoted to producing it. Hammering (tarq) is the term applied to the technique of hammering annealed metal into flat sheets to a uniform thickness. The sheets are then cut into the required shapes for bending, decorating, and/or soldering.

All the decorative metal-working techniques used today were developed in the ancient world, but the ancients had to use bronze and flint instead of the high tensile steel tools that are available today. One of the oldest techniques is repoussé, which requires blunt chisels or traces to systematically punch out a scribed design. Although fine tools are available on the Peninsula, Bedouin jewellery silversmiths still work with fairly crude implements.

Embossing (*zakhrafa*) and repoussé (*buruz*) are decorative techniques in which the design, or domed pattern or shape, is hammered out from the back of a thin piece of metal. The sheet is first laid upside down on a bed of pitch mixed with fine sand or ash, or a shaped mould and then the desired patterns are beaten out with punches of various shapes. Sometimes an object is filled with pitch instead. Because the pitch mixture is yielding by nature, it allows the metal to follow the contours encouraged by the tools. Pitch, being a tacky substance, also serves to hold a metal sheet in place. The metal is released by warming the pitch. Annealing is carried out at intervals during the repoussé and embossing processes to keep the metal malleable. Some of the finest examples of ancient repoussé were made in Ur, Mesopotamia (circa 2500 BC).

Metal was also stamped to shape for jewellery in

the ancient world. Stamping is the mass-production method for repoussé or embossing and it was developed at about the same time. Although repoussé is a demanding, laborious and time-consuming technique in comparison with stamping, production of the bronze stamp itself required an advanced degree of tool-making skill. There is, as yet, no evidence of stamping to produce Bedouin jewellery in Arabia. Stamping is a short cut to reproducing shallow repetitive designs and a means of achieving an exact copy at speed. This is also a benefit of casting but repoussé has the advantage of requiring less metal.

Some Bedouin ear-rings and nose-rings owe their beauty to the painstaking technique of repoussé. The work is often so fine as to resemble, at a glance, the technique of granulation – the edges of half-moon-shaped ornaments are punched from the back to create a delicate beaded border. The worked sheet of metal is fixed to a plain metal backing and the two parts are then soldered together. The domed backs of scarab beetle-shaped pendants are created in this fashion.

Most round objects, such as large beads, hollow charm cases and bracelets are made by embossing. To make a bead or ball, two discs of metal are beaten to form two halves. For some pieces, it is necessary to make two different shapes – the

second is fashioned over a mould of reverse shape to the first to create the opposite half of the object. The two pieces are then soldered together. This ancient method has remained popular through the ages because solid cast objects use too much metal – and it can be mastered by machinery.

Until the technique of soldering was developed, early craftsmen joined metal by riveting, pinning or literally sewing it with wire. Apart from being aesthetically displeasing the rivets, pins and threads made weak links.

Like most of ancient man's achievements, soldering may have been a chance discovery. The key to joining separate pieces of gold lay in the level of impurity present in the precious metal being worked. When it was alloyed with another metal (usually silver or copper) the proportion of impurity always varied in proportion to the time it took to melt. An observant craftsman long ago must have noticed that gold of one colour melted more quickly than that of another, and flowed readily establishing a join. This particular type of gold was thus isolated and thereafter used specifically for joining – an early form of soldering. It is impossible to tell whether craftsmen grasped the connection between impurity and melting point and thus alloyed the gold deliberately or whether they merely selected a low-melting gold

Left: *To make wire, the silversmith must first cut flat sheets of metal into thin strips. These strips are then beaten to roundness before the drawplate is introduced. Thin strips of metal are also required to make beaded wire. This is, in the case of Bedouin jewellery, very narrow strips that have been corrugated by blows from a punch. The regular ridging can give the appearance of fused-on tiny spheres but it takes much less work. Most shapes are edged with beaded wire today, and it is used to create segments on a spherical bead and cover joins, and circle cylindrical hirz ends.*

Left: *These pictures show strips of metal being cut into squares, and these tiny pieces being applied to a newly-made cylindrical charm case to accent an all-over pattern of fused granules. Filigree is used less and less because it is a very exacting technique beyond the abilities of most of the silversmiths in Arabia today. The small square pieces are easily produced and look quite attractive when turned sideways and applied as a diamond shape. This shape was popular with silversmiths in the past but was made up of two triangles, usually formed with a coarse form of granulation. Small spheres of metal could be stacked pyramid-fashion along the edge of a domed half of a silver bead. When the two halves met, diamonds were formed from the meeting triangles. Triangles of stacked granules were once prevalent on the silversmith's work but these, too, take more time than today's craftsmen are prepared to devote.*

by its colour. Pure gold is a bright, clear yellow; the various shades seen today are purposely achieved by modern jewellers by the addition of base metal and silver.

Satisfactory soldering (*liham*) was achieved only after the development of a flux. Soldering is generally called "hard soldering" in reference to assembling the basic parts of a piece of jewellery. The metal used to join the pieces of an ornament is similar in appearance to the metal in the pieces, but it must be alloyed at a lower melting point. Bedouin jewellers usually add copper and zinc. As gold and silver are heated and approach melting point, the metal develops a skin of oxide that interferes with the flow and adhesion of the solder. The surfaces to be soldered, therefore, must be coated with a flux. This prevents oxidization through contact with the air and, as only coated surfaces will receive it, the flux guides the solder to the points to be joined. Borax is a

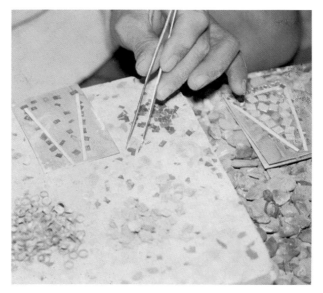

Left: *Each silversmith has his own method for making traditional jewellery. Some seem quite unorthodox. The triangle shape is perhaps the most prevalent and it is used as a pendant for both an* ilagah *and a* qiladah. *This silversmith appears to be attempting a matched pair of triangles which suggests they will be for* ilagahs *– one is worn each side of the face. Shapes are usually cut first and then the embellishment is applied and fused. In this case, the craftsman intends to cut out the shapes after he has embellished his pieces.*

commonly employed flux.

Fusing (*sahr*) is another method of amalgamating two metal objects into one. this technique also requires melting metal with intense heat, but copper carbonate is employed instead of flux. This joining technique is required for fine filigreed wire work and for affixing tiny metal granules and shapes as it allows the embellishment to adhere cleanly to a plain surface. Fusing is a simple term for a very complicated technique similar to that used for granulation and requires great skill. The methods of fusing gold once employed by Bedouin jewellers produced an effect resembling brilliant Etruscan work. The technique seen on later examples is crude in comparison.

The techniques of chasing (*naqsh*) and engraving (*hafr*) are often confused because they create a similar effect. The chasing tool makes an indentation pushing metal to one side without loss, whereas engraving involves actually gouging out metal with a sharp tool. Chasing is a decorative technique in which the design is struck on metal by blows from a punch on the front of an ornament. Decorative punches can be used with this technique to achieve a repeated pattern. There are two types of chasing – flat and repoussé. Flat chasing decorates the front of a piece of smooth metal. Repoussé chasing is applied to the front

surface in the same manner, but it brings out the detail of a raised pattern that has been previously beaten or embossed from the back. Skilful chasing is sometimes used in conjunction with engraving to achieve extremely beautiful floral motifs and geometric designs on Bedouin jewellery.

Engraving is quite different from other decorative techniques. It is often used immediately after hammering, prior to shaping and soldering. Engraving is done by working the surface of the metal with a sharp pointed tool called a graver. This gives a clean, sensitive line most suited to delicate, linear floral patterns. Well-executed engraving is an exquisite enhancement for fine silver and is sometimes used on Koranic amulets. Crude but effective designs are achieved by scoring the surface with geometric designs or by gouging out a repeated simple motif. Although bronze tools are not hard enough, examples of engraving from the Bronze Age have been found. Since iron tools were not introduced until 900 to 600 BC, the engraving implement was probably a sharp sliver of flint.

Granulation (*habbiyat* or *shugl al khurduq*) is the art of applying minute metal grains, known as shot, to a metal surface to produce a three-dimensional decorative effect. It is one of the most difficult and painstaking ornamental techniques requiring the tiny spheres of metal to be arranged

Above left: *The crescent shape is almost as popular as the triangle for a motif on Arabian Bedouin jewellery. It is seen still on modern gold jewellery. Whatever the shape, it is an Arabian custom to draw attention to it – the decoration never crosses the shape but rather, the beaded wire, filigree or granulation follow the outline. Inside this work, tiny granules, shapes, and shapes made from filigree can be seen in scattered fashion or in a more restrained application drawing attention to set stones.*

Above: *Tweezers held in one hand and a blow torch in the other, the silversmith fuses tiny diamond shapes to figure eight links. He works on slabs of stone – quenching the metal in water is not considered as suitable as slow cooling on stone. Their equipment is crude but they manage remarkably well.*

113

with tweezers on an object and then fused to its surface. Richly-embellished surfaces on Arabian ornaments echo Egyptian jewellery taken from tombs of the Pharaohs; yet, in the case of granulation, the technique is believed to have evolved with the Greeks and developed with the Etruscans.

Granulation is the most remarkable of all the metal-working techniques devised by ancient goldsmiths. Although it was comparatively crude when originally employed in the third millennium BC, it reached technical perfection by the eighth and seventh centuries BC. The incredibly fine granulated ornaments of the Etruscans presented a puzzle for the modern world. Centuries after the technique's demise, craftsmen endeavoured to reproduce granulation, without success until an English metallurgist, H.A.P. Litterdale, devised the technique of colloidal hard soldering. This produced results close to those achieved by the ancients. Litterdale decided to omit the use of flux in favour of a copper hydroxide paste upon which the tiny granules were arranged. When this medium was heated, it decomposed into copper oxide and then into copper to form an invisible join between the granule and the surface being decorated. Still, one cannot be sure this method was the one used by craftsmen in antiquity. It was a delicate and skilled process involving the individual arrangement of spheres measuring 1/10th mm. It is no wonder that jewellers continue to marvel at the exquisite workmanship of the Etruscans. In the modern world, fine jewellery with granulation is produced on the island of Bali.

When the Etruscan culture was absorbed by Rome, the art of granulation was largely replaced by that of filigree so wire became important to the jewellery craft. Wire (*silk*), has a long history as a practical and decorative element of jewellery. The early production of wire must have presented ancient jewellers with many problems and there are various theories about how they coped. It is generally agreed that the first step in manufacture was cutting out thin strips of metal with a chisel. Some ancient craftsmen hammered these strips into roundness or rolled them between bronze plates. Sometimes, thick wire was fashioned by casting. Hollow wire was formed by twisting gold strips around a mandrel which was afterwards withdrawn. In any case, it was difficult to make wire of an even gauge by these methods.

The use of twisted wire in jewellery was popular with the Greeks and later the Romans and it was the latter who eventually evolved the drawplate. The drawplate provides a method by which wire can be tugged through a series of successively smaller holes until reduced to the required even gauge. Byzantium, a combination of Greek culture and Roman administration, developed the use of wire for ornamentation and carried it forward into the age of Islam. The Arabian silversmiths continue to use the drawplate and Bedouin jewellery makes much use of wire. It is often plaited or woven in loose or tight weave; sometimes two pieces of wire are merely twisted together for use as applied filigree. Wire is also required for making filigree à jour and various styles of chain.

Chain-making (*amal silsilah*) is yet another technique for working silver. Hand-made chain (*sil-*

silah) is a principal element of Bedouin jewellery and often the major part of an ornament. Bedouin chained ornaments are constructed with many different types of links, spacers and baubles, sometimes combining the techniques of filigree, granulation and sand-casting. The plainer, more crudely executed types of chain, illustrate the earliest use of wire which developed into a series of simple connections to link baubles together.

Low-grade silver is invariably used for chains, presumably because silver becomes stronger when alloyed with a baser metal. This assumption would seem to be reasonable, as original intact ornaments often have high-grade silver pendants that contrast greatly with the poor quality silver of their supporting chains.

Because most Bedouin silversmiths usually work alone today, without the aid of apprentices, they normally set aside sufficient chain for their future needs, just as they stock modest quantities of other

components for their most popular pieces.

Filigree (*mushabbak*) is a decorative technique that can be executed in two ways – à jour or applied. A jour ("open" like lace) is a highly ornamental technique achieved by twisting and forming wire into delicate patterns that are then soldered or fused for solidity. In the applied method, the twisted wire patterns are usually cleanly fused to the ornament rather than soldered. The variations of applied filigree in Bedouin jewellery includes tightly twisted lengths of wire placed to accentuate shape and short sections twisted to form tiny circles which are scattered over a surface. The applied method of filigree is more commonly employed by Bedouin jewellery craftsmen.

Wire in itself was not only a remarkably useful achievement but its invention also lent enormous scope to jewellery decoration. Early craftsmen used bronze tweezers to fashion their wire decoration. The ancient Greeks were expert with filigree and favoured such delicate and detailed decoration in preference to gems for jewellery embellishment. A great deal of Arabian Bedouin jewellery also reflects this preference.

Wrought metal (*madan mutarraz*) is metal worked into shape by twisting or bending after being made malleable by annealing. Many heavy Bedouin

Below: The most common style of silver waistbelt, produced in Riyadh today, is one which appears to have evolved from a southern belt. The silversmiths who make it are Yemenis, and the old silver belts sold in the Riyadh Women's souq are rarely similar. Further evidence is provided by ornaments from Yemen which are made the same way. The silversmith here works on a short length to make a belt of the same style shown on the right. He extends this length link by link – this flexible belt is made up of hundreds of meshed links overlaid with small metal squares placed diamond-fashion. The surface of the diamonds bears a punched pattern. Mounts for red stones are usually soldered along the belt at regular intervals and a fringe of chains with pendant bells is added to the bottom edge. Silver belts with chased or engraved designs are very rare – the embellishment is usually applied and confined to fused-on filigree and granulation. Coins and stones are frequently added and set in high collets.

bracelets are wrought and the finest use of this technique can be seen in the twisted "Celtic" style from central Arabia.

Casting is an extravagant technique and was therefore rarely used in ancient times. Nevertheless, it was mastered more than 5,000 years ago.

Open casting is the simplest form whereby a shape is chiselled out of stone or baked clay and filled with molten metal. It was quite satisfactory for flat objects such as spearheads and axes. Objects made in this way have been recovered in Mesopotamia and date from around 3500 BC.

The piece mould, still in use today, came about when three-dimensional objects were required. The subject was first modelled in wax and then coated with clay that was cut open when dry and emptied of wax. The mould could then be reassembled and filled with molten metal. The resultant object was, of course, very heavy and the method wasteful. The more economical method of hollow casting involved suspending a solid core in the centre of the mould and allowing the molten metal to flow around this core.

The most sophisticated method of casting to be evolved was *cire perdue* (lost wax casting). Here again, the object would be modelled in wax and covered in clay – except for one vent. When the clay was hard, the mould would be heated and the wax melt and flow out. The hollow mould could then be filled with molten metal to achieve perfectly smooth objects without join marks. Objects created by *cire perdue* were found in the tomb of the Egyptian Pharaoh Tutankhamen (1350 BC).

Sand-casting (*sakb*) has been used on the Peninsula but is not as popular as other Arabian jewellery manufacturing methods because it makes an extravagant use of metal. Yet, the technique is still used in the Middle East because it reproduces a three-dimensional object accurately and rapidly – and inexpensively so far as labour cost is involved.

To produce a sand-cast object, the jeweller first makes a mould by pressing the model between a pair of heavy frames that are packed tightly with very fine sand. The frames are then divided and the model removed. After treating the sand with a mixture of alum, salt and sugar in water to preserve the impression, the mould is reassembled and molten metal poured through an opening previously prepared for the purpose. When the cast copy is removed, the mould is discarded because it can be used only once. When the object cools, excess metal is removed and finishing touches are made. This kind of casting can be done successfully only if the model is relatively simple and has no undercuts.

Whatever the silversmithing technique, final cleansing is essential to a well-finished piece of jewellery. The Bedouin jewellery craftsman removes excess solder by soaking the objects in diluted sulphuric acid or an alum solution. The metal is then brushed with pumice powder and polished with a brass brush. Final burnishing is done with a cloth.

At Faw, in the north-west corner of the Empty Quarter, small iron crucibles have been found. These are dated between first–third century AD. Although the ancient Arabians who used this equipment, possessed faceted gems and beads,

there is no evidence of gem cutting as a developed industry on the Arabian Peninsula as yet.

It is interesting to note that the first jewellers in remote antiquity were lapidaries – man has been polishing, shaping and drilling stone since Neolithic times. However, the earliest gemstones, instantly beautiful, required no work. An appreciation for minerals can be seen in the hoard of pretty stones found in Peking Man's cave where they were stored about half a million years ago. In time, when man came to desire body adornment for reasons other than warmth or protection, he turned similar stones into jewellery. Fifteen-thousand-year-old Danish graves have yielded strung amber, which may have been the first bead material because it is soft and easy to drill.

The stone-cutting and metal-working crafts eventually came together; today some of the most artistic modern jewellers train as lapidaries as well as goldsmiths. For many in the lapidary craft,

Below: The beauty of the craftsman's final product depends on cleansing. He appears to be as delighted as his audience with the finished product. From the moment that the silversmith begins work on the glowing silver bar until this stage, the ornament's component parts have been ugly – discoloured, rough and dull. The metal seems far removed from precious. The pieces are soaked in a stripping solution and then scrubbed and finally polished. The liquid is sufficient to remove the roughness as well as the inevitable grime that collects in the crevices due to blowing sand.

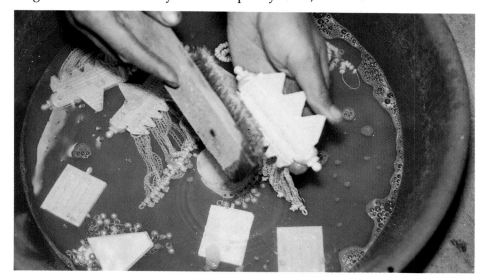

Above: *A Jeddah silversmith proudly laid out his latest creation and instructively set beside it an old example of the same style. This traditional* necklace *is still popular and it has not been reproduced in gold, although the same design elements can be seen in the new gold. A traditional* piece *can be large or small, in fine silver or poor, exhibiting a silversmith's individuality, and remain a recognizable standard style.*

115

faceting a gem is the ultimate achievement.

A lapidary's art includes the cutting, polishing and general shaping of a gemstone (*jauharah*) for ornamental use. Although quite different from a gemologist, he relies greatly on the science of gemology, for he must know a gemstone's true identity and characteristics to know how it is going to behave.

Stone cutting as an art is believed to have originated among the ancient Babylonians and Egyptians and gradually advanced until it reached excellence in ancient Greece and Rome. Cut gems appear in Arabian Bedouin jewellery, but the stones are generally imported. The gemstones set in old Bedouin jewellery are customarily in flat form; red stones are an exception, often appearing fashioned in different ways, either cabochon, faceted or engraved. The cabochon and faceted cuts are the most important methods for fashioning gems and the more commonly seen of the three techniques used for these red stones.

The word "cabochon" refers to the rounded top of the stone and comes from Old French: "cabo", meaning "head". It is a style developed mainly to prepare gemstones to fit standard mountings. There are three forms of cabochon. The highest dome is called "double cabochon", the most common medium dome is called "high cabochon" and the shallow dome is termed "tallow-topped". This cabochon shape is prevalent in Roman rings and remains the most popular cut for garnets set in Arabian Bedouin jewellery. Turquoise commonly appears around the world cut as a cabochon, but is rarely so in Bedouin ornaments. It is common practice everywhere to use this cut for stones whose true beauty is not dependent upon faceting as in the case of the diamond.

The greatest progress in stone cutting occurred during the seventeenth century and the reflective and sparkling properties of gemstones were improved as lapidary work was advanced. The most significant development was the improved understanding of the optical properties of gems. It is believed this knowledge was introduced from India, where the Mughal rulers had huge deposits of precious stones. The rose cut was developed and later the fifty-eight faceted brilliant cut. The latter method exploited the diamond's ability to refract and reflect light – a quality which had lain hidden with the cabochon cut and barely touched by the rose cut. All stones became increasingly important features in jewellery from this time – the diamond becoming the most prized and maintaining ascendancy.

In 1770, George Ravenscroft developed a new strong, dense glass by using lead. It has all the properties of a diamond except hardness and became known as "paste" or "strass" after a French court jeweller who did much to promote fake gems. These fake gems were often hand cut. Bedouin jewellery makes much use of fake gems and occasionally they are faceted.

Faceting, like all gemstone cutting (*qat jauharah*), consists of grinding and polishing gemstones with successively finer grades of abrasives and, to do it well requires great skill. Lapidaries have been faceting gemstones by methods that have changed little over hundreds of years for the finest and

most valuable gems were almost always cut this way as faceted planes made maximum use of the optical properties of the gemstone.

Intaglio, the name given to an engraved stone, involves a design that has been sunk into the surface, unlike the cameo where the background of the subject is cut away. The Greeks were the finest exponents of intaglio in the ancient world and it is recorded that they began engraving (*mahfur*) hard stones in the fourth century BC. The Greeks passed their skill on to the Romans who developed intaglio into an even greater art form.

Engraved red stones are occasionally seen in traditional Bedouin jewellery, and their designs were perhaps once symbolic. Large reddish stones (sometimes carnelian or garnet) are usually inscribed "Allah". The garnet (*aqiq ahmar*), being hard and durable, is a most worthy subject for the engraver's skill.

The bonding agent used by Bedouin jewellery craftsmen to set gems is pitch, a black or dark brown tenacious, resinous substance – the residue from distillation of tar or turpentine. It is hard when cold but becomes semi-liquid when heated. Pitch has been used since ancient times. It is believed the pitch was taken from natural seepages on the Arabian Peninsula.

Above: *Archaeological evidence reveals that ancient jewellery craftsmen worked in small booths throughout the Middle East, just as they often do today. The Arabian silversmiths who produce traditional Bedouin jewellery can still be found thus in many parts of the Peninsula, sitting cross-legged and fashioning metal into ornaments. Today, many artisans are retiring and the younger generation are turning to more profitable occupations. Their booths are being torn down as they become vacant, and the space is filled with new jewellery shops aglow with modern gold. Perhaps one day the craft will be revived to the former high standard, and new technology will provide ways for traditional Arabian Bedouin jewellery to be produced economically and well, thereby gaining the attention it deserves.*

List of Technical Terms

آجور : أشغال معادن مثقبة .

À jour: A style of metal-work that is open like lace

تعويذه : هو شيئ يلبسه الشخص معتقدا أنه يحميه من الشيطان .

Amulet: Object, commonly known as a charm, worn in the belief that it will protect the wearer· from evil.

تلدين : تلدين المعدن لإزالة هشاشته وجعله قابلا للطرق بواسطة التسخين ثم التبريد .

Annealing: Technique for softening, removing brittleness and making metal malleable for working by alternately heating and cooling

أرابيسك : طريقة الزخرفة الاسلامية وتعتمد على الأشكال الهندسية أو الخطوط المنحنية ، وأحيانا تحتوي على الأوراق والزهور والحيوانات .

Arabesque: Islamic style of decoration based on either pure geometric relations or endlessly flowing curvilinears, sometimes incorporating leaves, flowers and animals

معايره : تحديد درجة نقاوة المعدن .

Assay: Test for metals to ensure standard fineness

لؤلؤة باروكيه : لؤلؤة غير منتظمة الشكل .

Baroque pearl: Pearl of irregular shape

موضع الفص من الخاتم : الجزء العلوي من الخاتم حيث يركب الفص .

Bezel: Upper part of a finger-ring, usually supporting a stone

كابشون : حجركريم بدون سطوح وله شكل مقبب .

Cabochon: Gemstone shaped and polished without facets, and domed in appearance

كاميو : صدفه أو حجر ذو نقش بارز.

Cameo: Shell or stone carved with a relief design, opposite of intaglio

صب : تشكيل المعدن بصهره وصبه في قالب .

Casting: Shaping of metal by pouring it in molten state into a mould

خزف : مادة تصنع من الطفل وتحرق في فرن وغالبا ما يجري صقلها .

Ceramic: Pottery made from clay and fired in a kiln – often glazed

ترصيع : هو من فنون الزخرفة على المعادن ، حيث يحفر الرسم على المعدن بواسطة حركات المثقب على الوجه الأمامي ، وهناك نوعان من الترصيع منبسط ، وفيه بروز.

Chasing: A decorative metal-working technique where the design is traced out by blows of a punch from the front. The two kinds of chasing are flat and repoussé

سيرى بردو: طريقة صب ، يوضع فيها نموذج من الشمع في الرمل ثم يصب المعدن المصهور ليحل محل الشمع ، وتسمى أيضا طريقة الشمع المفقود .

Cire perdue: Casting technique where a wax model is placed in packed sand. The molten metal is poured into the mould replacing the wax which melts away. Also called the lost wax process

التجزيع : طريقة تستعمل فيها شرائط معدنية رفيعة يتم ثنيها لتكون خلايا ثم تلحم وتطلى بالمينا .

Cloisonné: Technique where narrow strips of metal are bent to form cells which are soldered to a base and filled with enamel

طوق معدني : هو شريط طوقي أو شقه خلفية تشكل موضعا أو مكانا لحجر. وغالبا ما تكون على شكل مخالب .

Collet: Encompassing band or ringed flange forming setting or socket for a stone, often partially filed away to make claws

تاج : إطار مرصع أو غير مرصع بالجواهر يلبس على الرأس .

Diadem: Jewelled or plain band worn around the head, once a badge of royalty or distinction

صفيحة السحب : لوح من معدن صلب يستخدم لتثبيت قوالب سحب الأسلاك .

Draw-plate: Piece of hard metal with holes of varying sizes through which wire is tugged. As successively smaller holes are used, the wire eventually reaches the required even gauge

إلكتروم : سبيكة طبيعية من الذهب والفضه .

Electrum: Natural alloy of gold and silver

117

Embossing: Similar to repoussé. A process of raising a domed shape on the front of the metal by beating it with punches and a hammer from behind

النقش البارز: طريقة زخرفة وفيها يطرق الشكل على ظهر اللوح المعدني حتى يبرز الشكل على وجه اللوح المعدني .

Engraving: Technique for cutting patterns in a metal surface using a sharp tool called a graver

الحفـر: هي قطع زخارف على سطح المعدن بواسطة استعمال أداة حادة .

Facet: Plain surface on a gem that is cut to reflect light

السطيح : سطح صغير على حجر كريم يتم عمله لعكس الضوء .

Faience: Term conventionally used for an ancient glazed composition with a quartz base. Also a term applied to glazed earthenware

خزف مزخرف : إصطلاح يطلق على المادة المصقولة القديمه ولها قاعدة من الكوارتز، كما يطلق أيضا على الآنية الخزفية المزخرفه .

Filigree: Ornamental wire-work formed into delicate tracery in two forms: either applied, i.e. soldered to a metal background or left as openwork, à jour

صياغة تخريمية : شغل زخرفي بالأسلاك يتحول إلى زخرفة تشجيريه ، وهي إما تلحم بخلفيه معدنيه ، أو تترك مفتوحه مثل الآجور .

Finial: Cap of a pinnacle

قمة مزخرفه : مثل قمة البرج .

Flux: Fusing agent such as borax used in the soldering process to omit oxidization through contact with the air and thus to facilitate adhesion; also to guide solder to the points to be joined

مساعد صهر: مادة مثل البوراكس تستعمل أثناء عملية اللحام لمنع الأكسدة وبذلك تساعد على اللحام ، وكذلك لإرشاد اللحام إلى الأماكن التي سيجري لحمها .

Fusing: Technique for amalgamating two metal objects into one by melting with intense heat, using copper carbonate

الصهر: هو عملية دمج جسمين من المعدن بحيث يصبحان جسما واحدا وذلك بواسطة الصهر تحت درجات حراره عاليه وإستعمال كربونات النحاس .

Gem: An object fashioned from a gemstone

الجوهره : هي الجسم الذي صنع من حجر كريم .

Gemstone: Treasured mineral found in the earth, including the organic compound amber and non-minerals such as coral, pearl, jet and so on

الحجر الكريم : جسم معدني كريم يوجد في الأرض ، ويشمل أيضا العمبر وهو مادة عضويه ، وكذلك بعض المواد غير المعدنيه مثل المرجان واللؤلؤ والكهرمان .

Glass: Non-crystalline solid substance made by fusing sand with soda or potash, or both, often including additional ingredients

الزجاج : مادة صلبة غير متبلوره تصنع بواسطة صهر الرمل مع الصودا أو البوتاس أوكليهما مع مركبات أخرى .

Granulation: Minute spheres or grains of metal fused to a flat metal surface to produce decoration in relief

التحبيب : كرات دقيقه أوحبيبات من المعدن مثبتة على سطح معدني مستوٍ لإخراج زينة سطح بارزه .

Hammering: Technique of hammering annealed metal into flat sheets in preparation for cutting and shaping

الطرق : اصطلاح يطلق على عملية طرق المعدن اللدن إلى صفائح مستويه قبل القطع والتشكيل .

Intaglio: Engraved stone, a carved design being hollowed out of the surface, the opposite of a cameo where the background is carved away

النقش الغائر : حجر محفور بحيث يكون الشكل غائرا في السطح ، عكس كاميو.

Jewel: Ornament worn for personal adornment usually containing stones or a gem that has been prepared for mounting

الجوهره : ١- حليه تلبس للزينة وتحتوي عادة على حجر. ٢- جوهرة مجهزة للتركيب .

Lapidary: One who cuts gemstones, excluding diamonds

صاقل الجواهر : هو الذي يقطع الأحجار الكريمه باستثناء الماس .

Mandrel: Round metal rod for winding thin metal to create hollow wire or rod around which metal is forged or shaped

عمود دوران المخرطه : قضيب معدني يستخدم في إنتاج أسلاك مجوفه أو قضيب تشكل حوله المعادن .

Matrix: Mother rock in which gemstones are found

متركس : الصخور التي يوجد بها الأحجار الكريمه .

Mineral: Compound or element occurring naturally as a product of inorganic processes

المعدن : أي عنصر أو مركب يوجد في الأرض بشكل طبيعي نتيجة للعمليات غير العضويه .

الصدف

Mop: Jeweller's term for *nacre*. See *nacre*

الصدف : الجزء الداخلي من المحار .

Nacre: Iridescent lining of a group of molluscs which yield pearls. Also known as mother-of-pearl

النل : خليط معدني أسود اللون ويتكون من الكبريت والفضه وبعض المعادن الأخرى .

Niello: A composition of a metallic black appearance made from sulphur, silver and other metals, and used as enamel

غير معدني : وتشمل المواد العضويه مثل اللؤلؤ والمرجان والكهرمان .

Non-mineral: Organic fossils including pearls, coral, jet etc

الأشياء النفيسه : وتشمل الأصداف والأحجار وغيرها .

Objets trouvés: French: "found objects" such as shells, seeds, stones and so on

النحت : هي الطريقة التي تعطي نماذج مفتوحه بإستعمال إزميل .

Opus interassile: Technique where an open pattern is pierced in metal with a chisel rather than a saw

المعجون : زجاج يستخدم لتقليد الأحجار الكريمة .

Paste: Glass used to imitate precious stones

المعالجه : طريقة معالجة الجواهر المعدنية ، وتسمى أحيانا المعالجة البيضاء ، وهي آخر مرحلة في صناعة المجوهرات ويتم فيها تنظيف الجوهره بغمرها في محلول مخفف من حامض الكبريتيك أو محلول الأوليم الساخن ثم الصقل ببودرة الخفاف .

Pickling: A process of treating metal jewellery. Sometimes called "white pickling". The last step in the jewellery-making process, designed for general cleaning, as it removes excess solder. The object is soaked in diluted sulphuric acid or a hot alum solution; a final brushing with pumice powder, an abrasive, follows

الطرق الخلفي : طريقة زخرفه وفيها يطرق الشكل من ظهر اللوح المعدني حتى يبرز الشكل على وجه اللوح المعدني .

Repoussé: Decorative technique for working sheet metal, where the design is hammered out from behind with punches, to raise a pattern which stands out in relief on the front

الطوق : طوق خاتم الإصبع .

Shank: The hoop of a finger-ring

الخردق : حبيبات صغيرة من المعدن تحضر بواسطة تسخين قطعة من المعدن حتى درجة الانصهار ثم تحويله إلى حبيبات صغيره .

Shot: Minute grains of metal achieved by heating a metal fragment to melting point. This separates into many spheres on a moving surface

الكتف : قطعة من المعدن مثبتة في طوق وموضع الفص في خاتم الإصبع .

Shoulder: Piece of metal attached to both shank and bezel of a finger-ring

اللحام : طريقة تثبيت الأجزاء الأساسية للجوهرة بإستخدام المادة المساعدة على الصهر والمعدن الذي له درجة إنصهار منخفضة عن الحليه .

Soldering: Technique for assembling the basic parts of a piece of jewellery, employing flux, and similar metal to the pieces to be joined but one which is alloyed to a lower melting point than the ornament

فلكه مباعده : قضيب مخرم على مسافات متباعده .

Spacer: Separating bead or bar pierced at intervals, and threaded to ensure that multiple strands of beads and links remain correctly spaced in relation to each other

حجر : اصطلاح يطلق على الأحجار الكريمه ، الجوهره ، الحليه ، والحلى المزيفه .

Stone: Term applied to a gemstone, a gem, a jewel and fake jewels

الطلسم : تعويذه تلبس بإعتقاد أنها سوف تحمي الشخص الذي يلبسها أو تجلب له الحظ السعيد والصحه والقوة .

Talisman: Object worn in the belief that it will protect the wearer or bring him good fortune, health or strength

النهايه : نهاية التوكه أو السوار أو الخلخال أو الحبة النهائية في العقد .

Terminal: End of a torque, bracelet, armlet or anklet and the end bead in a necklace

المعدن المطاوع : يطلق هذا الوصف على أي معدن يمكن تحويله إلى معدن مطاوع وبذلك يمكن طرقه أو لفه أو ثنيه .

Wrought metal: Metal worked into shape by twisting or bending after being made malleable

Materials

The materials employed to create Arabian jewellery long ago were probably taken from the earth close by the silversmith. This theory is strengthened by the fact that carnelian is typical of southern Arabian jewellery and turquoise (which usually appears alongside copper) is prevalent in the more northern regions of the Peninsula.

Although Arabia has always imported gems and metals, it is a richly endowed land. Gus van Beek writes that brass objects first appeared in southern Arabia in the first century BC, some certainly being imported but others probably being made locally.

Historically, brass was an alloy of copper with zinc and tin, bronze being copper and tin only. Today, this yellow alloy is usually copper with zinc alone – a third of the total weight being zinc. Sources of copper in the past were found within the Arabian Peninsula and to the north at the head of the Gulf of Aqaba.

In the 1930s, American engineer H.K. Twitchell was invited to Arabia to investigate the country's water potential. During this visit, he happened to see a bag of rocks from western Arabia that appeared to be rich mineral ore. Assay confirmed that this ore was indeed incredibly rich and subsequent mining at Mahd al Dhahab by the Saudi Arabian Mining Syndicate (SAMS) between 1939 and 1954 produced 765,768 fine ounces of gold and 1,002,029 ounces of silver. The United States Geological Survey's 1975 report, *The Geology and Ore Deposits of the Mahd al Dhahab District, Kingdom of Saudi Arabia*, states that this area is the most productive within the Kingdom. The name Mahd al Dhahab means ''Cradle of Gold'', which could be freely translated as ''Mother Lode''.

The radiocarbon method of dating known as ''carbon-14'' used on slag at this ancient mining site indicated that the mines were functioning during two periods in the Peninsula's early history. Carbon from the older slag indicated a date of about 1000 BC, whereas carbon from other suggested the period 750–1258 AD. No production records are available for these early operations. However, when SAMS began mining there in 1939, it was estimated that nearly 1,000,000 short tons of tailings and dumps were piled around the old workings. SAMS treated about 293,848 tons of these discards which yielded about 0.62 ounces of gold per ton. This inferred that even higher grade material was treated in the ancient mines. As the early miners had worked only to a depth of eighty-five metres, it was expected that rich ore would be found deeper underground. Subsequently, this has proved to be the case.

Most Bedouin jewellery is fashioned from silver and one question commonly raised about these ornaments concerns the source of the silver. One explanation is that Maria Theresa *talers*, Turkish silver majeedis and other ''trade dollars'' were melted down to provide metal. It is obvious, however, from the amount of jewellery available that this source cannot have been the only one. Sufficient coins would not have remained for transactions. Any additional quantities could have been imported. In all likelihood, the metals required to make Arabian jewellery were supplied from a number of places outside the Peninsula and entered by various ports. This speculation is borne out by the fact that Arabian mines have been reopened only in this century after hundreds of years of inactivity. Yet, since it is known that Bedouin silver ornaments have been re-created many times, perhaps some of the silver content may have come from ancient yields. There remains a romantic mystery which may one day be solved.

The study of coins has led to the development of a method that can, in fact, accurately determine the silver source. It was necessary to damage a coin to analyse its metal content until a method was developed at the University of Michigan. The technique requires only a tiny rubbing to be taken from the edge of the coin on a piece of roughened high-purity quartz. This quartz is then irradiated with neutrons from a nuclear reactor and the metal made radioactive. From the types and amounts of radioactivity found on the quartz, it is possible to determine the fineness of the coin sampled and to discover the amounts of impurities present. Ancient and medieval metallurgists did not realize that many silver sources contained as much as one percent gold as an impurity and therefore did not attempt to remove this precious constituent. Each silver source has its own characteristic level of gold impurity which was unaltered by early crude silver-refining processes. Thus, the level of impurities in old silver coins can provide valuable historical information. For example, two silver coins may appear to be made of identical silver but analysis may reveal a different mother lode. This method could be applied to the oldest surviving examples of Arabian Bedouin jewellery and perhaps permit the determination of the actual source of silver used for these ornaments.

The suggestion that some of the silver in Arabian Bedouin jewellery came from Mahd al Dhahab could be confirmed only if ornaments that were many hundreds of years old still existed, and this is most improbable as silver perishes. It is feasible that pieces available today do contain a proportion of silver from ancient Arabian yields, such as Mahd al Dhahab and Samrah. Samrah, located in central Arabia, ceased operation about 800 AD. Silver has also been found in the west and in southern and eastern parts of the Arabian Shield.

Standard silver has 925 parts pure silver to seventy-five parts alloyed base metal (for a total of 1,000). It is characterized in a pure state by its lustrous white colour and great malleability and ductility.

People who possess silver, whether it be fine

"sterling" or excellent to inexpensive "plated" are generally quite ignorant about it. This is a lamentable state because some knowledge about the properties of silver is vital to its preservation. Silver should be kept from the air as much as possible and proper care involves the regular removal of tarnish. Silver is softer yet less malleable than gold and also less stable; it corrodes quite readily and tarnishes when exposed to sulphur compounds in the air. Although as much silver jewellery as gold may have been made in the ancient world, it cannot be proven because most pieces have perished.

While silver (*fiddah*) must be separated from the other constituents of the mined ore, gold (*dhahab*), is sometimes found alone. The natural alloy of silver and gold (electrum) was thought by the ancient Greeks to be a separate metal and silver as a pure element was discovered accidentally as a by-product of the gold-refining process.

The most common question asked about Bedouin jewellery is whether the silver is "real". Most traditional Bedouin jewellery does contain silver, but the alloy ratio varies greatly from piece to piece. Silver objects are usually made of an alloy; pure silver is rare – as it is soft, the craftsman adds base metal to make the item durable. He prefers to use copper because it gives the best sheen. "Sterling" silver is made to a strict formula laid down by experts; objects stamped "Sterling" should be of high silver content (92·5 percent), rendered adequately durable by the addition of copper. Genuine sterling silver pieces are hallmarked by an assay office as a guarantee of quality and adherence to the prescribed formula. Bedouin jewellery is never hallmarked, although it sometimes carries the stamp of the silversmith. Bedouin jewellery is not normally plated but in recent years, silversmiths have dipped base metal pieces in liquid silver. This imparts a garish finish.

A collector will learn to recognize high or low silver content in Bedouin jewellery by handling pieces and becoming familiar with them. The higher the silver content, the richer the sheen and the more velvety the touch. Shallow designs incised or punched into high-quality silver pieces are quite often worn away because of the softness of such high-grade silver. Despite this damage, the smooth and silky patina that remains is very beautiful and easy to recognize. The more lead-like the appearance of the ornament, the less silver therein. In fact, some pieces could be termed "cupro" or "German silver" because there is almost no precious metal present. Cupro is an alloy of seventy-five percent copper and twenty-five percent nickel, and German silver is an alloy of copper, nickel and zinc. Both are lightweight but resemble silver.

Despite the custom of melting down Bedouin jewellery on the death of its owner, new ornaments re-created from the old metal may appear to be identical to the originals because of the preference for traditional designs and styles. However, it is possible that, with each successive melting, more base metal is added, and of course, the workmanship may be better or worse. A collector of Bedouin silver jewellery seeks the optimum combination – the best examples of traditional pieces, the highest silver content and the most accomplished workmanship. The weight of an object should also be observed carefully – two items may look identical in every way, but one may contain more metal and will therefore be more valuable. The same rules apply to buying old gold jewellery.

While three precious metals – platinum, silver and gold – are the ·foundation of the jeweller's craft, it is gold that takes the predominant position. Apart from being appreciated for its beauty and rarity, gold (*dhahab*) is the metal-worker's ideal medium, for it is the most malleable, ductile and durable of materials. A goldsmith (*sayegh al dhahab*) may draw it into wire as fine as a hair or beat it into leaf so thin that the light will shine through. It may be cast with a finger print or smelted into minute spheres.

It is supposed that gold was first discovered in the sixth millennium BC from alluvial deposits. It is found all over the world and every race (with the exception of the New Zealand Maori) has shown interest in it. The chief gold sources today are South Africa, Australia and Russia.

Pure gold is too soft for ornaments, so it is usually hardened with silver, copper, palladium or nickel. The proportion of gold in an alloy is measured in karats (kt) – pure gold being assessed at 24 kt. In its pure state, gold is remarkably stable and impervious to the ordinary processes of corrosion and decay; a gold coin can lie buried for eons and still appear as if newly minted. Because of its incorruptibility, gold has long been associated with eternal life.

Bedouin jewellery, although predominantly silver, traditionally includes some gold ornaments. The embellishment techniques are generally limited to hammering and embossing to make curved, flat sheets and granulation and filigree for surface decoration. The Ashanti of neighbouring Africa are perhaps the best known for beaten gold ornaments, although they did not make as great a use of set gems like the Egyptians.

Some Bedouin ornaments are brass (*nahas asfar*) which seems to be employed as a yellow metal substitute for gold. This theory is supported by the jeweller's custom of catering to the needs of the poorer Bedouin as well as the rich. Moreover, the conclusion is borne out by the fact that a traditional oval forehead ornament, usually made from gold and displaying set turquoise with garnets and pendant pearls, are occasionally made of brass.

Gemstones

Precious gems are generally minerals, but out of 3,000 kinds, only about seventy have ever been regarded as gemstones. These, however, have been constant for thousands of years.

Initially, it may have been the colour of certain minerals that attracted primitive man. Possibly their specific characteristics led them to be highly valued and, in earliest times, gemstones were hoarded purely for treasure.

It is known that early man revered gemstones – possibly because he was in awe of the similarly beautiful sun, moon, stars and sky. The wearing of *objets trouvés* probably came about when he observed how nature's seasons adorned the landscape – just as nature provided the guidelines for males to wear jewellery.

Eventually, gemstones were acquired for religious and superstitious purposes as well. In time, they became valued for dynastic purposes as Crown Jewels and curses were often attributed to great stones. In medicine, too, gemstones found a place and some were associated with astrology. Today, precious stones are applied in technology and worn as birthstones.

Ornaments have magical significance when the wearer has faith in the object's ability to protect or to heal. Sometimes, he believes that the form, colour or constituent elements of the amulet convey a sort of wisdom. Magical properties have long been attributed to jewels and precious stones, partly because, according to the lore of contagious magic, anything worn close to the body was assumed to affect its wearer's health. Today, in the Western world, some doctors recommend that patients wear copper bracelets (sometimes inset with magnets) for relief from rheumatism, and small amounts of gold in solution are injected to relieve arthritis. The American Indian has always believed in the ability of copper worn next to the skin to relieve pain. Copper, a malleable, adaptable metallic element of yellowish-red colour, was probably the first metal worked by man. It is alloyed to produce bronze and brass and appears in at least 240 minerals. The fine colour of a gemstone is often attributable to copper. Because of its high conductivity, copper is used extensively in the electrical industry. The Chinese believe the human body is controlled by electricity and their medical treatment of acupuncture successfully relies upon this theory. It is possible, therefore, that contact with certain minerals aids the human body. Certainly, it has been proved that minerals included in tonics and taken medicinally are beneficial.

Body ornament was an integral part of man's earliest religions. No doubt the beautiful minerals found in the dust were quickly associated with the great mystery of life as heavenly symbols. Superstitions have attached themselves to many famous stones, as well as to certain minerals, but this may be the result of collected statistics – a set of incidents that seem to convey a pattern. Most probably the beliefs owe everything to gossip.

Precious stones have been copied no less than anything else of great value. The history of imitation and fake gems is long; jewel substitutes were used by the Egyptians, Greeks, Romans and Phoenicians, although not as efficiently as they are today. There are ways to detect imitation gems but the only sure method is to remove the stone from its setting and put it to the test prescribed by gemologists for the analysis of that particular gem. However, a keen eye together with some basic knowledge will sometimes provide the correct answer. Such can be the case with the average jeweller who is rarely a gemologist. The gemologist's science is concerned with investigating and establishing facts about gems and gemstones. As the laws and procedures applied to the study of minerals fit gemstones perfectly, any trained mineralogist can easily become a competent gemologist. Because gemstones are of monetary value, proper identification is crucial. In analysing gems and jewels the chemical composition, internal structure, light characteristics and other physical peculiarities such as hardness are important factors to be considered.

Confusion has arisen on occasions in the basic vocabulary of gemology. Paul Desautels, Curator of Gems and Minerals for the Smithsonian Institution, writes "'Gemstones' are the specially treasured minerals found in the earth and 'gems' are the objects fashioned from them; 'jewels' are gems that have been prepared for mounting in jewellery or other works of art". However, historically, a "jewel" is also any piece of jewellery with or without a set gem.

Jewels are measured by weight, and the basic unit is a carat (ct), a word derived from "carob", the small Oriental bean remarkable for its uniformity of size and once used for weighing precious metal and gems. A carat (ct) is $\frac{1}{142}$ of an ounce or 200 milligrams. The carat weight is often described as $\frac{1}{5}$ of a gramme – subdivided into 100 points. This measure is not to be confused with karat (kt), referring to the fineness of gold.

Archaeological evidence traces the existence of the gem trade routes to a pre-dynastic period well before 5000 BC. Certain non-minerals – coral, pearl and ivory – joined the organic compound amber to become an accepted part of the Earth's treasury of gems.

Jade, rock crystal, steatite and lapis luzuli beads have been found at ancient sites in the Arabian Peninsula, but are no longer used in Arabian body ornament. Amber, coral, garnet and turquoise, in contrast, have remained popular there for 2,000 years.

The tendency to attribute powers to certain stones was often the reason for a specific selection. For example, green stones were believed by the ancients to prevent disease; red stones were reserved for the alleviation of bleeding and inflammation; and agate was worn to make the wearer agreeable and more persuasive. Amethyst was chosen to ward off intoxication, whereas malachite was used as a local anaesthetic or worn as protection against malign enchantment. Sapphire (the emblem of chastity), often chosen as an alternative engagement gem to the diamond (the symbol of eternity), was once considered to be a cure for boils. The practice of relating a gemstone to the birth month of its wearer is relatively recent, having been introduced sometime in the eighteenth century. As first conceived, the custom allowed an individual to receive the virtues of all the stones by changing ornaments as the months changed. Gradually, emphasis shifted to one stone only – to represent the birth month of the wearer. This was supposed to bestow an extra measure of its virtues upon him. Man still pays economic homage to these old traditions.

Turquoise

The word "turquoise" is derived from the fact that the finest blue Persian gemstone (from Khorasan) was exported through Turkey; the French called it "Turkish stone" or *pierre turquoise*. The ancient names for turquoise were *callais* and *callaite*. It registers 6 on the Mohs scale of hardness.

Many magical properties have been attributed to gemstones through the ages and perhaps turquoise is a leader in this field. It is said turquoise will glow when its wearer is content and will lose its sheen when she is sad. Hindu mystics suggest turquoise for money-raising. They recommend staring long and hard at a new moon and then immediately transferring this gaze to a fine turquoise. Enormous wealth, will come in due course. In the Western world, many possess this stone in the hope of forthcoming prosperity, and, as wealth itself, turquoise has been hoarded and used as currency. Turquoise is believed to be a powerful agent in reconciling quarrelling lovers and ensuring the wearer's fidelity – turquoise often appeared in Russian wedding rings.

Although the making of American Indian silver and turquoise jewellery is a relatively new craft, the American Indians have honoured the stone for centuries, some calling it *chal-cui-hui-tal*, the highest and most valuable thing in the world. Medicine men, hunters and warriors considered it indispensable. A turquoise attached to an arrow or bow was supposed to ensure perfect aim. Many Mediterranean and Middle Eastern people, too, consider turquoise a protection from harm and even as a means of making camels, horses and donkeys sure-footed.

Turquoise can be fine and an unflawed "robin's-egg blue" or coarse and threaded with matrix. It is never transparent and is generally coarse-grained. In Arabian Bedouin jewellery, with rare exception, turquoise is merely shaped and used in flat form and raised to prominence by its setting.

To keep its original colour and sheen, turquoise should not come into contact with grease, oil, strong chemicals, excessive heat or unnecessary abrasion, for any such marring is irreversible. The greenish colour caused by contact with grease or oil is referred to as "cabbage". However, it is claimed that the palest colour may be improved by dipping the stone in blue wax.

The Egyptians' use of turquoise stretches back to remote antiquity. In 5300 BC, it was mined in the Sinai Peninsula near Serabit el Khadem. Hieroglyphs record that seven or eight thousand years ago, 8,000 men were involved in a great turquoise mining operation there. Turquoise was much favoured by the Chinese and the Aztecs, too, both for adornment and for religious purposes. There were major sources of turquoise in Persia, China and North America. The streaked form, turquoise matrix, seen in Bedouin jewellery, can be found around Medina on the Arabian Peninsula (matrix is the stone in which gemstone is found). Rey Urban, a Swedish silversmith whose work reflects the ultra-modern Scandinavian trends, has noted that matrix turquoise is preferred by his clientele. Mexican and American Indian silver jewellery also suggests a preference for matrix turquoise.

The finest unflawed sky-blue turquoise comes today from the Nishapur district in Iran, as it has for many thousands of years. So perfect are these stones that it is difficult to tell them from fakes. No stone has been imitated with greater success. Ceramic and porcelain (*khazaf*) are commonly used, as well as plastic (*marin*), and, nowadays, turquoise dust can be bonded together with synthetic resin to achieve an excellent imitation.

Garnet

Garnets, commonly a rich ruby red, are often set in Bedouin jewellery and generally are used in conjunction with turquoise. Garnet is an inclusive name for a group of silicate minerals used in industry as well as jewellery-making. These minerals are characteristic of metamorphic rocks (that is, rocks that have undergone transformation by means of heat, pressure or other natural causes).

The name "garnet" is said to have been derived from the Latin *granum* meaning grain – perhaps because garnets occur frequently like grains in the surrounding rock. Another theory is that the name derives from its resemblance to the inner colour of a pomegranate. The Bedouin call garnets *aqiq ahmar*, a named shared with the carnelian, meaning "semi-precious stone". Garnets are beautiful, durable stones of high lustre and strong colour and are fairly hard, measuring 6½–7½ on the Mohs scale.

Garnets rose to prominence as a jewel with the Romans of the first century AD. They were fashionable in the Victorian age, too. Garnet-encrusted jewellery is currently made in Czechoslovakia, but the stones are small; a few being the fine, deep ruby colour common to Victorian jewellery. Most newly mined garnets are more brownish, indicating that the ruby-red colour is becoming rare. It is a relatively abundant stone, comprising several different sub-species which are not always red; the green demantoid garnet, for instance, is a most valuable stone. Because large garnets are becoming increasingly rare, collectors purchase old jewellery. A brownish-pink variety comes from the gravel beds of Sri Lanka and from exposed veins on the Arabian Peninsula. Of the wide variety of garnet in the world, perhaps the best known comes from a large area near Trebenice in the Bohemian region of Czechoslovakia.

Carnelian

Carnelian (also known as Cornelian) is a brownish-red semi-transparent stone that is used interchangeably with garnet and red glass in Bedouin jewellery. It has been known and appreciated for thousands of years. Carnelian (aqiq ahmar), measures 6½ on the Mohs scale of hardness and is a quartz, as are most of the stones used in jewellery. The cryptocrystalline or fine-grained variety of quartz is known as chalcedony, and grouped under this heading are agate, onyx, chrysoprase, moss agate, jasper and tiger's eye, as well as carnelian. It is the colour zoning, caused by trace elements, or inclusions, that determine this categorization.

On the Arabian Peninsula, chalcedony is often called "the Medina stone", most probably because a great deal of it can be found there. Most certainly, western Arabia has long been a source of semi-precious stones. It is also common to the south-western and southern regions. Throughout Arabia, one can purchase loose or strung chalcedony in a variety of pretty colours, but these are from Pakistan. Many of the stones are flawed and pitted but a few exhibit the fine qualities for which chalcedony is known. The warmth of beautiful carnelian makes it stand out from the rest and explains why it was prized by the ancients; yet, strangely, it commands a trifling price today.

Carnelian is often a glowing orange-red colour, which can be imitated in glass, although bubbles are invariably present in such imitations. Carnelian, like turquoise, was mined on the Sinai Peninsula in ancient times. Many carnelian beads, some hand-painted, have been found at ancient sites on the Peninsula.

Amber

Sixty to seventy million years ago, soft gluey resin oozed from trees; it hardened, dropped to the ground and lay buried until discovered by early man. He was obviously captivated by the beauty of this material, which we know as amber (kahraman), for archaeologists claim that it was treasured in the Stone Age and worn as jewellery for thousands of years. Danish tribesman, 15,000 years ago, carved amber into beads and strung them into long necklaces. Hoards of amber ornaments were buried with their dead in the apparent hope that they would appease spirits in an after life.

Large amounts of amber were a regular part of early trade route treasure and often cost as much as gold. In the Middle Ages, this esteemed commodity reached a peak of popularity and again was priced with precious metals. It has been used not only ornamentally but also as a gemological remedy, both internally and externally since about 9000 BC. Roman physicians often prescribed ointment made from ground amber as a salve for wounds. It was prized by the ancient Greeks not least for its magnetic properties which are manifested when rubbed; in fact, the word "electric" was coined from the Greek for amber, elektron.

For centuries, the most highly prized amber came from the Baltic coast in what is now Russia. The Romans called Baltic amber "gold of the north", but the location of the cache remained a secret until the Phoenicians visited the area in about 1000 BC.

Amber is a mineral organic compound – a fossil resin of the pine trees that flourished in the Tertiary period. It is found anywhere in the world where such resin-producing trees grew. Amber occurs as irregular nodules, rods or drop-like shapes in all shades of yellow to yellowish-brown. Light-coloured opaque material is known as "bone amber". Deeply-coloured translucent to transparent amber is prized as gem material. Although amber and amber-like resins have been found all over the world, true amber, succinite (characterized by its yield of from 3–8% of succinic acid) comes only from the shores of the Baltic and in the greatest amount from the glauconite sands or "blue earth" of the Samland peninsula in the Soviet Union. Other ambers contain little or no succinic acid.

Amber is a paradoxical substance – light enough to withstand the ravages of time and yet soft enough to be shaped by the simplest tools. Unlike other fossil materials, however, amber is not actually petrified. It remains the same organic material that flowed from those pines of long ago. The pressure of ice and immersion in sea water caused the molecules to rearrange themselves and polymerize, changing the resin from a tacky substance to a solid.

Legend asserted that amber was the solidified urine of the lynx (dark for the male, pale for the female) or the petrified tears of God. According to Greek myth, amber was the congealed tears of Phaethon's sisters who were turned to trees while weeping over his death. It was the Roman author Pliny, in 77 AD, who first described amber as a product of the plant world, yet amulets made of amber were worn by Roman women to protect them from witchcraft.

Ambers exist in many shades, from black to blue, green and red, to light golden brown and white. Quite often insects are trapped inside, perfectly preserved after millions of years. In the late 19th century, entomologists and botanists, inspired by Darwin's newly formulated theory of evolution, began to study these captives to learn about the flora and fauna of ancient forests.

Amber takes its name from the Spanish *ambar*, a rendering of the Arabic *anbar*, meaning a "combustible material". Amber is a very soft material (2½ on the Mohs scale) and burns with a bright flame. Its authenticity can be tested by setting it alight, but, as it floats in very salty water where imitations sink, flotation is a decidedly more satisfactory test. Jewellers recommend inserting a hot needle in the hole of an amber bead to ascertain if it can produce a burnt smell.

It is likely that much of the amber used in Bedouin jewellery found its way to the Peninsula through Afghanistan. The large cube-shaped amber beads common to Arabian Bedouin ornaments often seen in Morocco, North Africa, Qatar and Oman, as well as on the Peninsula, may be African amber, which until recently was used in Africa as trade beads. It usually ranges from opaque reddish brown to bright yellow – the red amber beads are said to have come from Germany long ago, although Simetite red amber comes from Sicily, Rumanite red amber comes from Rumania and Burmite red amber is found in Burma.

The simple tools of the amber-turner's trade have remained virtually unchanged for generations – a wheel (now motor-powered) and discs of stiff cloth mounted on a spindle serve the craftsman who holds the amber against the spinning cloth, turning it until the raw lump has been rubbed and shaped to the desired form and sheen. Amber beads on the Arabian Peninsula, are rarely spherical – they are usually oval or lozenge shaped and worn in long strands, generally without pendants or relief beads of other materials.

Coral

Coral, known as *marjan* in Arabic, is a non-mineral, along with jet and pearl. (Non-minerals represent less than ten percent of all gemstones.)

Coral was worn for wisdom long ago and, because of its beauty and rarity, it was included with gemstones. The Chinese credited coral with magical properties and it has been used for centuries as an amulet, a talisman and for ornamental purposes. The tales surrounding gemstones are indeed fascinating, but none more fanciful than the ancient Greeks' legendary explanation for coral. They believed it to be the hardened blood that dripped from the severed head of Medusa.

In reality coral is formed by large colonies of minute sea animals called polyps, which secrete a continuous hard skeleton of calcium carbonate.

Coral polyps lay down their limestone deposits in different patterns, according to their species, so that each type of coral has its own unique growth pattern. A wide selection of natural forms is appreciated as decorative household ornaments but few varieties are suitable for use in jewellery.

Robert Arndt writes "Coral reefs are the mightiest structures ever built by any life form on this planet. The small flower-like polyps are the architects and the landlords of their reefs for coral also shelters other animal species". Coral reefs occur in all the world's warm seas where conditions are right. In particular, water salinity must not be too high and water temperature must not vary too greatly during the year (55° to 60°F is ideal). The sea must be relatively quiet and clear enough to admit sunlight.

The different light requirements of each coral species have resulted in depth zonation for the species. Hawaiian coral, growing at levels too deep for divers, is recovered by submarines equipped with remote-controlled cutting devices. Because it takes up to fifty years for coral to reach maturity and seventy-five years to produce prime specimens, it is unlikely that coral will cease to be treasured; although, as man invents new methods for its recovery, much more coral may reach the market.

Malaysian, Japanese and Mediterranean waters supply most of the marketable coral. The finest gem coral is dredged off the coast of Algeria and Tunisia and at several points off the coasts of Italy, France and Spain. Mediterranean coral gathering is an Italian industry operating out of Naples, where coral from Japan and Malaysia is also fashioned.

The coral reefs of the Red Sea are famous for their variety and colour, although maritime industries such as coral digging, pearl fishing and sponge gathering have lapsed because of sudden storms and treacherous shoals. However, the sea also farms coral by tossing broken pieces upon the shore. The rough coral used in Bedouin jewellery is most likely from the Red Sea – although, according to shipping documents, worked coral and fake coral have been imported for over 100 years. The gathering of black coral from the Red Sea was once a thriving industry. This black coral (*yusr*) may have been used in the past in necklaces, but evidence suggests that it was reserved for export and for *mesbaha yusr* (black coral prayer beads).

As a gemstone, coral is easily worked, measuring 3 to 3½ on the Mohs scale. It became the height of fashion in the nineteenth century. Today, the palest pink variety, known as "angelskin", is highly prized and used by exclusive Western jewellers. The coral used in Bedouin jewellery is generally dark pink to red. Precious coral can range from pale pink to red and gem quality coral exists also in gold, white and black.

Imitations of coral are legion. It has been copied by many methods and imported into Arabia to be used equally alongside genuine coral, a fact that stresses the importance of a red bead of familiar traditional appearance in Bedouin jewellery. It is interesting that, in the jewellery trade, small pieces of thin branches of red coral, which are drilled down the centre and strung, are called "Arabian beads". Possibly the name derives from a time when Arab trade routes carried coral throughout the known world. Today, on a sidewalk in Jeddah, men from Chad in central Africa sell varying qualities of coral beads to a ready Western market. Although not of "gem quality", these pitted beads have appeal as well as a high price.

Pearl

In the past, the finest pearls in the world came from the Arabian Gulf, so it is not surprising that the finest old pieces of gold Bedouin jewellery should incorporate pearls (*lulu*). Arabian towns-women's jewellery, at the turn of the century, made use of pearls, too, and they were usually the same baroque seed type (*bezr*). These occasionally form multi-stranded necklaces with relief beads at regular intervals and cord ties. Arabian towns-women in the past were particularly fond of pearls – in the Hijaz, a bride was traditionally bedecked with many pearls and diamonds on her wedding day. Gertrude Bell noted that a Bedouin woman wore "ropes of bright pearls" in Hayil and Lady Anne Blunt, also visiting Hayil, wrote of head ornaments ending in long strings of pearls with bell-shaped gold and pearl tassels. "The pearls were irregular shapes and unsorted as to size and quality".

Today, the pearls used in Bedouin jewellery are often the cultured variety from Japan. In either case, the pearls are 'baroque'' (that is, of irregular shape). Strands of similar pearls from China are also sold today alongside Bedouin jewellery.

Pearls, like other non-mineral gems, have long been treasured by man and classified as precious on the grounds of their beauty and rarity, Nature creates a pearl when a grain of sand invades an oyster shell; irritation stimulates the mantle of the mollusc to pour out nacre, a fluid that encases the foreign material and leaves it as an excrescence on the lining of the shell.

To culture pearls, an incision is made in the mantle of the mollusc under aseptic conditions and a bead of freshwater mussel is inserted with a tiny graft of mantle. When the mollusc is returned to the sea, the bead is enveloped entirely and is eventually covered with nacre.

When cultured pearls first appeared in the 1930's, natural pearl prices collapsed, never to recover. Trading stopped overnight until some positive test could be devised that would distinguish between the two products of the oyster. Although X-ray may reveal the bead core of the cultured pearl, it is not a reliable guide. The pearling industry suffered further when much of its manpower was drawn off to the oilfields.

Myths surround pearls as they surround most precious stones. One of these tales, recorded as fact, suggests that Cleopatra (attempting to impress Mark Anthony) tossed a priceless pearl into her goblet and drank the contents once the pearl had dissolved. Experts say that any liquid capable of dissolving a pearl would have done damage to Cleopatra herself. Perhaps, then, she swallowed the pearl whole.

Another myth persisting into modern times concerns the care of pearls. It is said that pearls must be worn next to the skin constantly to retain their lustre and that royal families often requested their ladies-in-waiting to wear costly pearls for them, even to bed. In truth, to retain their beauty, pearls should be cleaned occasionally to remove damaging skin acids and they should not be exposed to prolonged heat or excessively dry air.

In past ages, pearls were often likened to tears and sometimes raindrops because of their appearance. The rarest and most sought-after shape for a real pearl was traditionally the sphere, but other shapes (including pear, seed, blister, button and baroque) lend themselves more to the jeweller's wider artistic scope. Pearls are found in many subtle colours including pink, grey, silver, yellow, green, bronze, blue, black, cream and white. This variety makes pearls a craftsman's delight.

The measure used for weighing pearls is the "grain", which equals ¼ of a carat, the carat being ⅕ of a gramme. Pearl ranks 3½ on the Mohs scale.

Agate

Agate is another popular gemstone that appears in strung bead form in Bedouin jewellery. The name "agate" is derived from the Greek *achates*, a small rivulet in Sicily from which ancient Greeks and Romans extracted the stone. Agate is known in Arabic as *aqiq* – the generic term for a semi-precious stone. Distinguished by irregular bands of colour, agate is easily counterfeited but imitations appear only occasionally in Bedouin jewellery because genuine agate is available from many sources.

Minerals are actually nothing rare or exceptional – the entire Earth's crust is made up of them. Scientifically, minerals are defined as chemically homogeneous, natural constituents of the Earth's crust. Certain minerals, however, do stand out; people admire them, collect them to enjoy their beauty, and wonder what forces were responsible for their formation. Agate is a very beautiful though inexpensive stone, which is often appreciated by people who collect mineral samples yet, curiously, it is generally despised by those who like jewellery.

Agate, like carnelian, is a chalcedony and falls into the crypto-crystalline or fine-grained category of quartz. Agates include any chalcedony that displays a pattern, usually in bands and circles. The banding is formed by seeping water which intermittently carries silica (dioxide of silicon), a whitish material, into holes and cracks in the matrix or mother rock. The silica remains and piles up layer upon layer through the ages until it eventually become agate. Variations in colour occur when the water combines other minerals with the silica.

As a gemstone agate ranks 6½ on the Mohs scale. It can be coloured quite easily and uninterestingly coloured agate is often dyed by jewellers to bring out beautiful patterns. Methods of treating its colour were known to the Romans.

Glass and Faience

Beads and set stones of glass (*zujaj*) and faience (*khazaf muzakhraf*) are important components of Bedouin jewellery. The Bedouin have always given equal preference to semi-precious stones and these lowly mediums.

Glass is a substance that is both brittle and hard (6 on the Mohs scale). It can be either transparent or opaque. People who collect fine glass and all who admire it consider this invention to be one of man's most exciting discoveries. Yet Western people rarely trouble to think about so familiar a material, and certainly most people today consider it too ordinary to be worn in jewellery. Paradoxically, glass experts still do not completely understand how it was first made, nor is it known exactly where or when, but most probably, it was an accident.

According to tradition, glass was discovered by chance when ship-wrecked Phoenician sailors noticed a vitreous material forming among the embers of their fire. There may be an element of truth in this myth, for the basic component of glass is sand (silica) which is fused with an alkaline substance (soda) and lime (calcium carbonate). All of these were present on the beach.

Glass has been known since the middle of the second millennium BC. It is generally agreed that glass-making began in one of the countries of the eastern Mediterranean. Long ago, the soda for glass-making was taken from seaweed or coastal plants which grow in abundance at the mouths of rivers of the eastern Mediterranean. Although the earliest surviving examples of glass have been discovered in Egypt, the art is thought to have reached there from Asia Minor. The ancient Egyptians, Phoenicians and Persians traded in primitive glass ornaments.

His Imperial Highness, Prince Takahito Mikasa of Japan writes, "I have no scholarly knowledge of glass; I am simply a layman who cries admiringly 'How beautiful!' whenever he sees fine ancient or modern works in glass". Prince Mikasa is particularly appreciative of ancient Persian glass, the existence of which was not confirmed until about 20 years ago when the Gilan Province tombs (northern Iran) yielded rich finds including beads. Unlike other glass objects, experts find it difficult to deduce the provenance of beads; because jewellery is made to be worn, it is carried from place to place. Despite this, a Japanese archaeologist, Professor Shinji Fukai, claims many of the beads found at Gilan are Persian and date from the first millennium BC. Identical beads as well as glass fragments – commonly referred to in Arabia as "Persian glass" – have also been found on the sites of ancient dwellings in eastern Arabia. Persian glass art flourished during the Sassanian period (226 to 642 AD) and continued into the Islamic period, when it came mostly from the Iranian highlands and Samarkand. Many glass ornaments and beads probably entered the Peninsula overland from the north.

At first glass was used to make ornaments. Glass pastes could be coloured and applied to small objects to make them look like precious stones. The paste could also be poured into terracotta moulds to make small statues, plaques and jewellery components. To make hollow objects, the paste was placed around moulds which could be broken later. This primitive glass paste was sometimes cut up into tiny pieces, which were pierced and then strung together. Larger objects could not be made until glass-makers had mastered the art of glass-blowing. This art is believed to have been developed in Syria late in the first millennium BC. Although it was a great advance, glass-blowing was also an accidental discovery, occurring when an unnamed experimenter dipped one end of an iron tube into a pot of molten glass and blew down the tube. The resulting glass bubble was the beginning of bottles and other thin hollow vessels.

Despite the fragility of glass, many ancient and beautiful objects have been preserved. Superb modern designs are made today in Scandinavia, while classical pieces are reproduced in Italy – both command very high prices. It is unfortunate that glass jewellery no longer receives the respect that it did in the past; yet, in time it may enjoy revived popularity, as have wooden beads for example.

Faience, the glazed pottery forerunner of glass, is a fused mixture of sand and lime covered with an alkaline glaze and an achievement of the ancient Egyptians. Using both of these mediums, Egyptians were able to imitate coloured gems at a relatively low cost. Glass, faience and substitute gems used in imitation of a gem are known as "paste" in English, while something of this nature is called *taqleed* in Arabic. The Bedouin woman would not be likely to apply this word to glass or imitation gems in traditional jewellery, however, because this would not be as important as it would be for the Westerner. Although fake gems and low-grade silver would affect the price when buying or selling her jewellery, the importance of possession with its complexities would count far more.

Gem Classification

Some collectors are determined to learn the exact nature of the stones set in their Bedouin jewellery. This is a pity because it means the stones must be prized from their settings. It is desirable to have the finest pieces possible for a collection, yet it should be remembered that, for the Bedouin woman, the quality of the stone was not as important as the traditional colour.

The most positive gem study techniques unfortunately involve destruction of the sample. Destructive tests, therefore, are generally reserved for uncut gemstones. Among such tests are chemical analysis, X-ray structure determination and the Mohs tests for hardness. Tests that are non-destructive include determination of refractive index, specific gravity, pleochroism, spectral pattern and examination for any foreign inclusions in the stone. These latter tests are generally quite adequate for correct analysis.

Because mineralogists and gemologists have perfected sophisticated instruments and non-destructive techniques, destructive analysis is a last resort – rarely can gem material perplex a competent man. Yet, man is also perfecting his ability to manufacture gemstones. This fact requires the science of gemology to maintain strict and thorough standards so that distinctions between natural and man-made gems are not obscured.

Refractive Index
When a beam of light hits the flat surface of a mineral at an angle, it bends, or refracts, as it enters the gem. If the direction of the light beam is slowly changed so that it strikes the surface of the gem at an increasingly lower angle, a point is eventually reached where it ceases to bend sufficiently to enter the gem and just grazes the surface. Any further lowering of the beam causes it to be totally reflected away from the gem. This is called the "critical angle" and differs with each gem substance according to its refracting ability.

An instrument known as a gem refractometer has been devised to quickly and easily measure this critical angle. The instrument usually contains a built-in scale indicating the refracting ability, or "refractive index", of the gem. To ascertain the index of a gem, one of the polished facets of the stone is placed against a mounting of highly refracting polished glass. Good contact is assured by placing a drop of special refracting liquid between the two surfaces. A light beam is brought through the glass to the gem. Light coming to the gem from an angle at which it will be refracted is bent into the gem, away from the instrument and is lost. Light coming in at any angle beyond the critical is reflected back into the instrument and hits the viewing eyepiece, its trace showing as a bright section on the scale. The numerical marking on the scale dividing the light portion (representing reflected light) and the dark portion (representing the light refracted into the gem) is the critical angle. For convenience, this measurement is numbered on the scale as the refractive index. The measurement is sufficiently precise that, by consulting a table listing the refractive indices of gemstones, one can usually make a quick identification of the gem in question. Synthetic gems, however, can also give a correct reading if they are made from the chips and dust of the mineral in question.

Specific Gravity
Specific gravity is the weight of a gem compared with the weight of an equal volume of water. To determine specific gravity, a gem is weighed accurately in air and weighed again while immersed in water. The "in water" weight is subtracted from the "in air" weight. The remainder gives the weight of a volume of water equal to the volume of the gem. This weight is then divided into the weight of the gem in air to find how many times it exceeds the weight of the water.

Pleochroism
Different colours can often be observed in a double refracting gem by looking at the gem from different directions. Any colour differences are recorded. This pleochroism, or dichroism, can be seen and the colours compared directly by using an instrument called a dichroscope.

Spectral Analysis
Spectral analysis of coloured gemstones (by a gem spectroscope) can supply useful information for identification. The spectroscope's function is to separate white light into its complete rainbow or spectrum of colours.

Inclusions
All gemstones under magnification reveal a myriad of inclusions. Even the "perfect" diamond has them, but it is ranked "perfect" if none are apparent when it is magnified ten times. With ten to forty times magnification, under a microscope, it is possible not only to identify the gem because of its characteristic inclusions but also to give its provenance, because "locality inclusions" are invariably present.

X-Ray
X-ray remains the most important single key to identification, but this valuable gemological asset requires the destruction of a small amount of the stone.

Care of Jewellery

Hardness

Gemstones are classified on a hardness scale; the softest quickly lose beauty when scratched or cracked. The most precious gemstone is often considered to be emerald, which is one of the most easily damaged. Although the diamond is sufficiently hard, lack of proper care may result in its loss from a damaged setting. Gemstones do break – sometimes from a blow or as a result of sudden, extreme cooling and heating.

The best way to define hardness is to consider the scratch-resisting ability of a gem. Since the early 1800s, a rough but convenient scale for measuring hardness (originated by the German mineralogist Friedrich Mohs) has been in general use. The Mohs scale is based on ten relatively common minerals which rank in order of increasing hardness:

1 talc	6 feldspar
2 gypsum	7 quartz
3 calcite	8 topaz
4 fluorite	9 corundum
5 apatite	10 diamond

The degree to which hardness increases between the numbers is not uniform. There is a greater degree of difference between the hardness of corundum and diamond (nine and ten on the scale) than there is between numbers one and nine. Almost all important gemstones are rated above six on this scale.

Owing to the conditions under which the Bedouin live, their jewellery (*jowaher*) has been subjected to excessive heat and dryness, abrasive dust and the body's acidic moisture – all of which tend to damage the ornaments. Professional cleaning at regular intervals is recommended for jewellery generally, but home care, painstakingly carried out, can suffice. The mildest effective cleaning abrasive for jewellery is toothpaste applied with a very soft natural bristle brush. Second-hand Bedouin jewellery often needs stronger treatment to remove imbedded grime. Soaking in baking soda is a good way to begin. A stiff brushing to follow will generally suffice before silver cleaning.

Silver polish is not ideal for intricate Bedouin jewellery, as any residue retained in the intricately embellished surfaces spoils the appearance of the jewellery. Although liquid silver dip is probably the most effective way of removing damaging tarnish from such surfaces, pieces must not be left in this strong liquid too long, and they must be rinsed thoroughly. If it is used, hollow objects are best brushed rather than immersed so as to avoid the chance of acid penetrating and perhaps remaining.

Liquid dishwashing soap and water are excellent for restoring gold to brightness and is ideal for use after liquid silver cleaning. The best method of preserving the brightness of silver, once is it cleaned, is to keep it from contact with the air – in order to prevent the ever-present oxides from setting up the tarnishing process again. It is purely a matter of preference, of course, whether to keep Bedouin jewellery highly polished or merely clean. Pieces of very fine silver respond well to liquid soap and water followed by burnishing with a soft cloth. Some collectors buff Bedouin jewellery with a brass-bristled brush. Jewellery, however, should be treated as something treasured and delicate. Individual pieces are best kept in separate containers, preferably lined with some soft material.

Bibliography

Aldred, Cyril *Jewels of the Pharaohs*, Ballantine Books, New York, 1978

Al-Farsy, Fouad Abdul-Salam, *Saudi Arabia – A Case Study in Development,* Stacey International, London, 1978

Anderson-Black, J, *History of Jewels,* Orbis Publishing, London, 1974

Aramco – Lebkicher, Roy; Rentz, George; Steineke, Max and other Aramco employees, *Aramco Handbook,* The Arabian American Oil Company, The Netherlands, 1960

Aramco – Lunde, Paul; Sabini, John A, *Aramco and its World,* The Arabian American Oil Company, Washington DC, 1980

Argenzio, Victor, *Fascination of Diamonds,* George Allen and Unwin, London, 1966

Arndt, Robert, Article: *Coral in the Gulf,* Aramco World Magazine, Nov/Dec 1978

Baumgartel, Elise J, *The Cultures of Prehistoric Egypt, Part II: Silver,* Oxford Univeristy Press for the Griffith Institute, 1960

Beresneva, L, *The Decorative and Applied Art of Turkmenia,* Aurora Art Publishers, Leningrad, 1976

Bibby, Geoffrey, *Looking for Dilmun,* Alfred Knopf Inc, New York, 1970

Blunt, Anne, *The Bedouins of the Euphrates,* Volumes 1 and 2, John Murray, London, 1879

Blunt, Anne, *Pilgrimage to Nejd,* Volumes 1 and 2, John Murray, London, 1881

Brijhushan, Jamilla, *Masterpieces of Indian Jewellery,* Taraporevala, Bombay, 1979

British Museum, *Jewellery Through 7,000 Years,* British Museum Publications, 1976

Burton, Richard, *The Gold Mines of Midian,* Falcon-Oleander, Cambridge, 1979

Clarke, Patti, *Jewellery in Easy Steps,* Studio Vista, London, 1977

d'Aulaire, Emily and Perola, Article: *Gold of the North,* Scanorama – Scandinavian Airlines Magazine, NAG Press Limited, 1978

Desautels, Paul E. The Smithsonian Institution, *Gem Kingdom,* Ridge Press, Random House Inc, New York

Dhamija, Jasleen, *Living Traditions of Iran's Crafts,* Vikas Publishing House, 1979

Dickson, H.R.P, *The Arab of the Desert,* George Allen and Unwin, London, 1952

Ernst, A, and Heiniger, Jean, *The Great Book of Jewels,* Edita, Lausanne, 1974

Fletcher, Lucinda, *Silver,* Orbis Publishing, London, 1975

Fukai, Shinji, *Persian Glass,* Weatherhill/Tankosha, NewNork/Tokyo/Kyoto, 1977

Gentille, Thomas, *Jewellery,* Pan Books, London, 1973

Ghantus, Leila, Article: *The Music of Arabia,* Ahlan Wasahlan, Saudi Arabian Airlines, No 2, Vol 1, Oct/Nov/Dec 1977

Gordus, Adon and Jeanne, Article: *There's Gold in them thar Coins,* L.S.A, University of Michigan publication, Spring 1977

Greene, Betty Patchin, Article: *A talk with Freya Stark,* Aramco World Magazine, Sept/Oct 1978

Hawley, Ruth, *Omani Silver,* Longman, London/New York, 1978

Hinks, Peter, *Jewellery,* The Hamlyn Publishing Group, London, 1969

Hoberman, Barry, Article: *Treasures of the North,* Aramco World Magazine, Sept/Oct 1979

Katakura, Motoko, *Bedouin Village,* University of Tokyo press, 1977

Kennedy, Sylvia, Article: *Iqd Mirjan – A Ceremonial Necklace from Yemen,* Quarterly: Ornament 4 (1), Los Angeles, 1979

Kuri, Zahi, Article: *Arabesque,* Ahlan Wasahlan, Saudi Arabian Airlines, No 1, Vol 2, Jan/Feb/Mar 1978

Khuri, Zahi, Article: *Arabesque,* Arab Esk Europe, The Netherlands, Nov/Dec 1980

Krause, Chester L. and Mishler, Clifford, *Standard Catalogue of World Coins,* 1979 edition.

Linecar, Howard, *Coins,* The Hamlyn Publishing Group, London, 1971

Luce, R.W; Bagdady, Abdulaziz; Roberts, R.J, *Geology and Ore Deposits of the Mahd Adh Dhahab District,* Saudi Arabian Projects Report, (IR-201 and 106; IR-195) prepared for the Director General of Mineral Resources, Ministry of Petroleum, Saudi Arabia, 1975

Mariacher, Giovanni, *Glass from Antiquity to the Renaissance,* The Hamlyn Publishing Group, London, 1970

McClure., H.A, *The Arabian Peninsula and Prehistoric Populations,* Study No 58, Field Research Projects, Ad Orientem, 1972

Michaud, Sabrina and Roland, Article: *Bold Horseman of the Steppes,* National Geographic Magazine, November 1973

Musil, Alois, *The Manners and Customs of the Rwalla Bedouins,* American Geographical Society, Oriental Explorations and Studies, No 6, 1928

O'Neill, Thomas J, Article: *Amber, Gold Window on the Past,* National Geographic Magazine, Vol 153, No 3, September 1977

Pesce, Angelo, *Jidda – Portrait of an Arabian City,* Falcon Press, Naples, 1974

Phillips, Wendell, *Oman,* Ministry of Information, Oman, 1972

Phillips, Wendell, *Unknown Oman,* Longman Group, London, 1971

Index

Figures in italics refer to illustrations

Platt, Nathaniel and Drummond, Muriel Jean, *Our World through the ages,* Prentice Hall Inc, New York, 1954

Richards, Alison and Sataloff, Joseph, *The Pleasure of Jewellery and Gemstones,* Octopus Books, London, 1974

Stillman, Y.K, *Palestinian Costume and Jewellery,* Museum of New Mexico and the International Folk Art Foundation, Sante Fe, 1979

Thesiger, Wilfred, *Arabian Sands,* Penguin Books, London, 1980

Thesiger, Wilfred, *The Marsh Arabs,* Longmans, Green and Company, London, 1964

Tordoff, William, *Ashanti under the Prempehs – 1888–1935,* Oxford University Press, 1965

Van Beek, Gus W, Article: *The Rise and Fall of Arabia Felix,* Scientific American, Vol 221, No 6, W.H. Freeman and Company, San Francisco, Dec 1969

Verband de Edelstein und Diamanten-industrie, *Edelstine – Precious Stones,* Schaefer and Schmidt, Germany, 1966

Vidal, F.S, *Pre-Islamic Burial Report,* translation of Arabic article, Al Manhal, Shaban 1375 – April 1956

Webster, Robert, *Gems in Jewellery,* Butterworth and Company, London, 1970

Weir, Shelagh, *The Bedouin,* Museum of Mankind, UK World of Islam Publishing Company, London, 1976

Willcox, Donald, *New Design in Jewellery – Scandinavia,* Van Nostrand Reinhold, 1970

Willis, Geoffrey, *Glass,* Orbis Publishing Limited, London, 1975

Wilson, A.J, Article: *Timna's Ancient Mining Secrets,* Optima – a review published by the Anglo American Corporation, De Beers and Charter Consolidated Groups of Companies

Winstone, H.V.F, *Gertrude Bell,* Jonathan Cape Limited, London, 1974